WHEN THE WAR ENDS

STUART CHASE has been commissioned by the Trustees of The Twentieth Century Fund to make a series of exploratory reports on postwar problems. These are being published under the general title, "When the War Ends," and the books are appearing at intervals during 1942, 1943 and 1944. The first volume, *The Road We Are Traveling: 1914-1942*, explored basic issues and fundamental trends; the second volume, *Goals for America: A Budget of Our Needs and Resources,* made some economic recommendations for the postwar United States. This volume, the third in the series, shows how our financial system operates and how it might be used to support full employment after the war is over. Later volumes will also examine specific questions of postwar readjustment. The list of titles follows:

WHERE'S THE MONEY COMING FROM?

PROBLEMS OF POSTWAR FINANCE

Guide lines to America's future

as reported to

THE TWENTIETH CENTURY FUND

by

STUART CHASE

NEW YORK

THE TWENTIETH CENTURY FUND

1943

First published November 1943
Reprinted November 1943
Third printing December 1943

MANUFACTURED IN THE UNITED STATES OF AMERICA
BY THE ACADEMY PRESS, NEW YORK

FOREWORD

M ONTHS BEFORE the United States went into the war, the Twentieth Century Fund decided to devote an increasingly large proportion of its resources to studying the problems of postwar readjustment. As a first step, the Fund retained Stuart Chase to write a series of books to give the public a stimulating and provocative picture of some of the problems which the United States will face "When the War Ends" (the title of the series). The entrance of the United States into the conflict has made these books even more timely. The first concern of everyone must be, of course, to win the war. But challenging objectives for the peace are dynamic aids to fighting morale.

The first volume of the series, *The Road We Are Traveling: 1914-1942,* was published in April 1942. It gave a moving and colorful picture of the revolutionary trends in our social and economic life which took place between the two world wars and laid down a sort of base line for a preview of the future. In the second book, *Goals for America: A Budget of Our Needs and Resources,* published in November 1942, Mr. Chase put into ringing words the demands which the American people are making for a better world after the war, and, using over-all figures of the goods and services these call for, he argued that we now have the resources to produce them. In the present volume Mr. Chase carries the discussion one step further. He maintains that, not only shall we have the man power and plant to meet these postwar demands, but we shall be able to finance that prodigious undertaking. In those volumes still to come Mr. Chase will face other problems involved in achieving a full employment economy after the war.

This series is designed to provoke thought and to stimulate discussion. Mr. Chase has been given entire freedom of authorship. However, he has had the advantage of advice and criticism in preparing the manuscript from the Fund's Economist, J. Frederic Dewhurst, and several other authorities—for which both Mr. Chase and the Fund are grateful. But the opinions and conclusions expressed in these books are those of Mr. Chase. The Trustees and Fund staff have taken no position either for or against them.

This series of books is one of several Fund publications in the field of postwar reconstruction. In May 1943 a second edition of the directory of national agencies engaged in postwar problems research and education was published under the title, *Postwar Planning in the United States: An Organization Directory* as well as a new study and discussion manual entitled *Wartime Facts and Postwar Problems,* designed to give the general reader a sort of descriptive catalogue of the profound changes that have taken place in our economy during the war and the specific problems of the peace which are likely to result. During the next few months the Fund will also publish a volume by Lewis L. Lorwin summarizing the postwar plans of governments and leading private agencies of all the United Nations. For publication in 1944 will be the results of a major investigation, now under way, designed to estimate, with as much precision and detail as may be possible, the needs and resources of the United States in the postwar world. This survey is being carried on by a special research staff under the direction of Dr. Dewhurst.

The Fund hopes that all these activities will contribute to a wide public understanding both of the unequaled opportunity of the postwar period and of the difficult problems it will present. The Fund is especially indebted to Mr. Chase for his challenging contribution to this end.

EVANS CLARK, *Executive Director*
The Twentieth Century Fund

330 WEST 42D STREET
NEW YORK 18, N.Y.
JULY 1943

CONTENTS

1

BEHIND THE DOLLARS

In 1925, Russia had been through a devastating war and a violent internal revolution. Her currency had been destroyed in a runaway price inflation, she was the world's worst financial risk abroad and she had very little gold. Yet by the end of the first Five Year Plan in 1933, Russia had invested some 60 billion rubles in factories, new cities, hydroelectric developments, armaments, houses, schools. There stood the new plant, ugly and solid. Without it Russia could never have met the onslaught of Hitler's armies.

Where did the money come from?

In 1933 it was freely prophesied that Italy could not invade Ethiopia. She had no credit abroad and almost no gold. The effort would bankrupt her. Italy went ahead, conquered Ethiopia, and emerged without financial collapse.

Where did the money come from?

Hitler took over a Germany which was technically bankrupt. It had defaulted on its foreign obligations. When he proposed to build a powerful army, together with all kinds of grandiose public works, he was laughed at in London and New York. Germany was insolvent, and the whole idea was preposterous. The nations of Europe which have trembled

under the thunder of panzer divisions know that Hitler built
even more terribly than he promised.

Where did the money come from?

When Japan began to rattle her sword in the direction of
Indo-China and challenge the United States and the British
Empire, wiseacres said it was a bluff. The long years of the
war in China had reduced the Japanese economy to a bag
of bones. She was bankrupt and could not sustain a real fight.
Yet she opened a new attack with devastating fury, and with
military equipment in planes, tanks, artillery, ships, that
was as excellent as it was unexpected.

Where did the money come from?

In 1939, the United States Congress declined to appropriate $4 billions for highways, conservation, hospitals, freight
cars, in the bitterly contested "lend-spend" bill. It was widely
held that the bill would lead to ruin and national bankruptcy.
Yet since the fall of France in 1940, Congress has appropriated almost $300 billions for armaments—seventy-five times
as much as the lend-spend bill—and a large fraction of it
has already gone into tanks and guns. Far from being ruined,
our national vitality has never been more vigorous, and great
financial moguls (see page 9) assure us that we shall be
able to swing the national debt.

Where did the money come from?

After the war America will need to maintain full employment, operate its industries at substantial capacity, provide
the essentials of life for all its own citizens, and help foreign peoples who are starving and unable to pay for the supplies. There will be a towering political demand for a world
delivered from chronic depression.

Where will the money come from?

It is clear from these examples that what a great nation can "afford" in periods of crisis depends not on its money but on its man power and its goods. Russia, Italy, Germany, Japan, the United States, all used money in the situations mentioned, but money was obviously not the dominant factor. Man power and materials were the dominant factor. Yet at other times, when crisis was not so acute, the money for necessary tasks could not be found. Unemployment, insecurity, want, dragged on. This is a puzzling paradox. At certain times a nation can afford what at other times, with no less money, it cannot afford. At certain times we are afraid of national bankruptcy, and at other times we give it hardly a thought.

Is there any way to smooth these ups and downs; any way to balance the things we can afford in terms of money with the things we can afford in man power and materials? The methods used in total war produce results but they are pretty rough ones, even in non-Axis nations. Can more gentle techniques be designed for peacetime which will also produce results? These are the questions we shall try to answer in this book.

The Disaster Economy

Adolf Berle tells of walking through a tenement district in New York with a friend a few years ago. What they see depresses them. They want to clean it up. But the moment they begin to think of ways to abolish slums, all kinds of difficulties loom across the path—the high cost of land, the difficulty of getting materials, exorbitant rates of interest, graft and corruption in the building trades, the avarice of landlords, the general apathy of everybody. As they walk along, listing the difficulties, any idea of improvement grows more and more remote.

But wouldn't a good, rousing earthquake solve everything? It would not only open up the ground, it would open up people's minds. The disaster would generate action, bold and immediate. The slums would be abolished once and for all. "Is it too much to ask that the driving quality which can be called forth by a great cataclysm might be made available for continuous and steady action? Is it necessary that some scourge of God, driving by brute fear, shall create a common will?"[1]

We recall the story of the man who was apprehended for going along the street smashing windows. He defended himself by saying it was good for trade. So it was—even if not for the owners of the buildings. If unemployment is rife, smashing windows, plowing under cotton, pouring milk into ditches, are all good—for trade. Even better is a raging flood, or a devastating hurricane.

For some years the potential output of the power age has tended to exceed the available cash in the hands of consumers. Gradually we have come to live in what might be called a "disaster economy," where waste and loss stimulate trade, where thrift and good quality depress it. Many examples come to mind. Advertising pressure has encouraged us to throw perfectly good things away and get a new model. The original AAA program was designed to boost prices and benefit trade by destroying crops. Long before the Triple A, a statue was erected to the boll weevil, one of the best things for trade that ever hit the cotton belt.

But the best thing of all for trade is war. In the United

1. A. A. Berle, Jr., *New Directions in the New World,* Harper, 1940.

States alone, the war has already provided an 80 billion dollar annual market, with $100 billions shortly to come. This terrific demand is running us into a man-power shortage in jig time. There are more orders on the books than there are men to fill them. Women, boys, old men, are being hauled in, but it looks now as if only a drastic conscription of labor can ease the shortage.

Conversely, we have the cynical phenomenon of "peace scares." Take this headline in the financial section of *The New York Times* for June 16, 1943:

PEACE TALK DEPRESSES COTTON
Rumors of Rumanian Feelers Send Futures Market Off 4-6 Points

With the fall of Mussolini, the New York stock market went into a nervous collapse. The good tidings were bad for trade. The financial editor of the *New York World-Telegram* wrote on July 27, 1943: "What the market said yesterday was that corporations, particularly those most heavily engaged in making war materials, will be unable to do as well financially in the postwar period as they have been doing in the last year or two. That is tantamount to saying that wars make for prosperity."

The Blight of Abundance

H. G. Wells has well summarized the situation in which abundance became a curse, and destruction a blessing to trade:[2]

The war [1914-1918] from the economic point of view had been the convulsive using up of an excess of production that the race had no other method of distributing and consuming. . . . The post-war increase in war production, which went on in spite of endless palavering about disarmament, did not destroy men, nor scrap and

2. H. G. Wells, *The Shape of Things to Come*, Macmillan, 1933.

destroy material, in sufficient quantity to relieve the situation. . . .
The more efficient the output, the fewer the wage-earners. The more
stuff there was, the fewer consumers there were. . . . This was the
paradox of overproduction which so troubled the writers and journal-
ists of the third decade of the twentieth century.

I don't believe that anybody likes this as a system, whatever temporary personal benefits glass dealers may get out of
smashed windows. It violates a deep human instinct. It makes
a mockery of the principle of "least work." Physical costs and
sacrifices are prodigious. While the efficiency engineers save a
few drops at the spigot, a torrent is rushing out of the bung-
hole. What is the use of making two blades grow where one
grew before when the whole crop may be burned or abandoned? An economy that relies for its stimulation on waste
and disaster is taking the road to oblivion as surely as the
dinosaurs, those creatures that were all bulk and no brains.

The so-called people's revolution springs, I believe, from
this paradox. The wayfaring man in every country is sick of
starving in the midst of plenty. The Germans' toleration of
Hitler was due to their blind hope that he could stop it.
Even war may seem preferable to rotting on the dole.

In 1931 the League of Nations reported thirty million unemployed in Europe and America. Trade, in fact, was bad.
What would be good for it? The most practical window-
smashing device was spending for armaments. Spending for
welfare projects ran into difficulties, as Mr. Berle noted, because such projects, it was feared, would not "pay out." But
nobody expects tanks to pay out. Therefore the opposition to
armament building in Europe was relatively mild. The tanks
were built with the labor of the unemployed. The vast rearmament program in the late 1930's did in fact end the de-

pression, but it filled Europe with guns pointing over every frontier.

When Production Outruns Consumption

One can begin to discover a rough cycle in the performance of the modern economy, where mass production outruns mass consumption. Machines grind and produce a mountain of goods. The goods pile up and presently choke the machines. The machines go on half time or stop altogether. The plethora of goods must be dynamited out of the way so that the machines can start again, and their human tenders can work again. Only total war has so far provided the requisite amount of dynamite.

Winston Churchill, in his book *The World Crisis,* vividly illustrates our point. He is speaking of the last Armistice Day on November 11, 1918.

A requisition for half a million houses would not have seemed more difficult to comply with than those we were already in process of executing for 100,000 aeroplanes, or 20,000 guns, or two million tons of projectiles. But a new set of conditions began to rule from 11 o'clock onward. The money cost, which had never been considered by us to be a factor capable of limiting the supply of the Armies, asserted a claim to priority from the moment the fighting stopped.

Instantly the problem of productive capacity and man power in excess of demand began to make itself felt. The "money cost" became a brake on the whole economic machine. A world "fit for heroes to live in" presently degenerated into a world of unemployment, doles and despair, the terrible world of J. B. Priestley's *English Journey.*

I have in my files pictures of veritable mountains of oranges, potatoes, coffee, marked for destruction. Nearly every farm crop has been plagued by surpluses since the last war. The great extension of wheat capacity in 1915-1919 produced not only ruinous postwar prices, but the dust bowl, where nature took a hand in helping trade by disaster. In the case of factories, the problem of surplus is present in the form of excess capacity, but mountains of unsold manufactured goods cannot often be photographed. A factory can close down faster than a growing crop.

If this is the sequence—I admit that it is a very rough description—what is the way to stop it? One obvious way would be to channel off the goods so promptly that they could not pile up to choke the machines. Indeed, short of war and disaster, is there any other way to make trade good? In simplest terms, this is the postwar economic problem. The channels for moving the goods are primarily financial, and the dams across the channels are financial—the "money costs" as Winston Churchill called them. They deserve the most cold and objective analysis, if we are to avoid the fate of the dinosaurs. What we need is the knowledge and the courage to organize our economy for full employment at a lower social cost. We shall never have full employment without effort, but we can surely have it without war and disaster and their toll of destruction, loss of freedom, and human lives.

2

ON D-DAY

THE BELLS WILL RING on Demobilization Day. Everybody will have a shout in his heart. But the American economic system will be a wonder to behold. It promises to look like something from the back of the moon. Any prophet who might have been bold enough to picture it in 1940 would have been run in by the police as mentally unbalanced. I remember the blank, terrified stares of a group of businessmen, when I ventured to say in 1940 that the national debt would presently go over $100 billions if the United States entered the war.

The National Debt

I was a rank conservative. When the war ends the national debt will stand at two to three hundred billion dollars, according to bank presidents, chiefs of great insurance companies, and other financial experts. What is even more astonishing, they seem to take the idea in their stride. To quote Emil Schram,[1] president of the New York Stock Exchange: "I am not appalled at the prospect. The American system is

1. *The New York Times*, April 19, 1942.

equal to any burden which it may have to carry." Myron F. Converse, former head of the National Association of Mutual Savings Banks, says that a public debt of $250 billions will not ruin the country if the national income remains above $100 billions, and affirms that we are going to hold it there under our present "managed money" methods.[2]

The National Income

British experience shows that the debt burden can be serviced without too much difficulty if it does not exceed twice the annual national income. In 1943 the national income in the United States will certainly reach $125 billions. By D-Day it may be running at the rate of $150 billions at 1943 prices. If prices have moved up by then, and they probably will move up further in a creeping inflation, the figure will be considerably higher measured in future dollars.

The War Output

The output for war goods and services is estimated at $80 billions for 1943. If the total national output in 1943 reaches $140 billions,[3] the war will thus be taking 57 per cent of American production. Where will the ratio stand on D-Day? I believe that 70 per cent is probably the limit, based on British and German experience. Donald Nelson looks

2. *New York World-Telegram,* May 7, 1942.

3. National output or national product or gross national income is a figure representing the value of all goods and services produced in the year. National income is always less than national output, for it does not include allowances for plant depreciation, mine depletion, corporate surpluses, etc. It represents the payments made to individuals during the year in the form of wages, salaries, professional and entrepreneural earnings, dividends, interest, farm income, etc. Neither figure can be taken as more than a rough measure of national welfare. See the excellent analysis of their limitations by Simon Kuznets, "National Income," in the *Encyclopaedia of the Social Sciences.*

forward to an annual war cost of $106 billions in the near future. This would be approximately 70 per cent of a national output of $150 billions.

These figures sound insane. When the National Survey of Potential Product Capacity estimated that we could produce $130 billions' worth of goods and services in 1929 dollars, the findings were laughed at as wildly and weirdly extravagant. Yet here we are, ahead of that volume, and destined to be far ahead of it by D-Day. None of us, not even the most starry-eyed dreamer, ever imagined the quantity of goods the American productive machine could fabricate once it was given a green light for full speed ahead.

War Taxes

Do you remember when a rise of 2 per cent in the income tax was considered practically confiscation? Our leading cartoonists blossomed forth with sketches of *homo Americanus* clad only in a barrel. Happy days! The 1942 rates would have caused apoplexy in many editorial chairs in 1940. As for the rates we can expect on D-Day, no substantial citizen could have looked at them and lived. Yet we shall pay them and live. Federal taxes are likely to amount to at least half the annual dollar cost of the war. If that cost is running at $100 billions, we shall be paying $50 billions in federal taxes.

Lend-Lease

In the last war we loaned some ten billion dollars to our allies, who defaulted on most of it. The unpaid war debts were an ugly political question for many years. Senators as well as common citizens found it difficult to see that our refusal to take large shipments of imports made it impossible for the allies to pay. We prevented them from paying by virtue of our high tariffs.

This time there will be no such debts—though I am not sure there will be no political arguments. Congress has already appropriated some $50 billions for lend-lease advances to the United Nations. In recent months we have been shipping as much as a billion dollars' worth of goods a month on this account.

It is the theory of lend-lease that such shipments do not constitute a formal loan in dollars, but rather an advance in goods and services, which, in due course, will be offset by goods, services or assistance remitted in return. Substantial offsets in the shape of food for our soldiers abroad are already being made.

The Banks

Long before D-Day, the banking system of the country has already become in a sense a ward of the federal government. Let Mr. Kiplinger, the famous business service man, describe the banks as they appear to him:[4]

Banks look the same on the outside as they did ten years ago. They have the same awesome fronts, the same barred windows and tellers' cages. But inside they are different. They look to government. . . . They get paid for following instructions, or "suggestions." The pay is the interest on the money they lend to government by buying the government's bonds. The pay amounts to a subsidy to banks. . . . The business of lending has become different. It already *has* become dominated by politics. . . . The war puts government firmly into the driver's seat as the general manager of the people's money, as the social director of the uses to which the people's savings shall be put. . . .

4. W. M. Kiplinger, *Washington Is Like That*, Harper, 1942.

Savings

The Department of Commerce, in a release in April 1943, estimated that savings in the hands of individuals will reach the unheard-of figure of $60 billions by January 1, 1945. The American people are getting more money in their pay envelopes than ever before in history. They cannot begin to spend it all. They have not points enough in their ration books. There are still many school teachers, farmers, workers, whose pay is below the average, and who are saving nothing, but they are offset by the new class of employees in war industries who draw more pay than they can dispose of. These savings could start a serious postwar inflation. If wisely managed, however, they can help cushion the shock of demobilization.

BACK OF THE MOON

The dollar figures mentioned earlier are necessarily guesses, but perhaps not too wild. Let us venture a few guesses about other aspects of the economy on D-Day.

There will be at least twelve million men in the armed services when the war ends, great numbers of them overseas. Most of them will have been out of touch with civilian work and civilian life for several years. Some younger men will never have had any regular job but fighting for their country. The whole force will have been extremely well cared for physically—the best of food, the sturdiest of clothing, the finest medical attention, every sort of equipment which their terrible tasks demand. They are already seeing much of the world. In many critical situations they are taking great responsibility. They are highly skilled in using the intricate machines of modern warfare. They feel that they *belong,* that they have a cardinal place in the American scheme of things. Certainly every speech they read or hear emphasizes the importance of that place.

When D-Day comes, most of these men will be glad to go home. But they will not, I think, be glad to sell apples on the street. They may not take kindly to being deprived of their high status in the community. They may not understand such treatment—and they promise to be very tough, well-disciplined and resourceful young men. We have never had such a terrific human force in our economy before. It is a force which will need to be treated with extreme consideration. Representative Dewey of Chicago knew what he was talking about when he said: "Local boards are drafting these boys into the Army. They will come back strong, lean, seeking opportunity and determined to have it. Why should they not find other boards ready to induct them into gainful enterprise? . . . If they don't, look out!"

I live twenty miles from Bridgeport. It had a terrific war boom in 1918, but that was nothing to the one it has now. Bridgeport never recovered from the devastating aftereffects of the first boom. Citizens looked forward with dread to another such fever. Now they have it, only worse. Bridgeport is but one of hundreds of American cities seized with munitions elephantiasis. On D-Day there they will be, helpless in their bloated immensity, their chief reason for existence gone or going. The workers in Bridgeport, like the men in the Army, have been given a vital feeling of belonging to the community. Like the men in the Army, they may not take kindly to being suddenly classed as untouchables at the bottom of the social pyramid.

Seventy Per Cent of Man Power

If the war ends with 70 per cent of our national effort going for military purposes, the man-power situation promises to look something like this:

		Per Cent
In the armed services	12,000,000	
In war industries and activities	33,000,000	
Total for war	45,000,000	70 [5]
In the civilian industries	20,000,000	30
Total national man power	65,000,000	100

Thus some 45 million citizens may be on the federal government's payroll—directly in the armed forces, indirectly in the war industries and services. The government cannot fire 70 per cent of the working population the way a meat market fires a butcher boy.

By D-Day the ranks of industrial labor may hold ten million women, boys and men not subject to the Army, who, if the war had not come, would be running their houses, playing bridge, living on investments, clerking in stores, studying in various schools, sunning themselves in Florida, or looking for a "respectable" job. The class structure of America has never been so rigid as that of Europe, but this wholesale migration by the middle class into the "proletariat" is something new under the sun.

My daughter went from her college commencement to a sanding machine with which she processed aluminum parts for fighter planes. In my little Connecticut town I can already count a score of professional and highly educated neighbors

5. In the second volume of this series, *Goals for America*, p. 116, the ratio was placed at 50 per cent. The march of events has made this figure obsolete.

who are getting themselves covered with grease on the night shift of Bridgeport factories. Suddenly, as history goes, a great segment of our population, well-educated and observant, finds itself faced with the problems of hours, wages, working conditions, safety—not by reading about such things at home, but by punching time clocks and standing in the assembly line. What is this likely to do to the official labor movement? It is likely to push it in two directions. On the one hand, it may make the closed shop far more difficult in many unions. On the other hand, it may make millions of Americans more sympathetic to the problems of individual workers. Women who used to keep two maids may learn how it feels to be bawled out by the foreman.

The Great Steam Roller

One by one the barriers which divide the wealthy from the poor will be lowered as D-Day approaches. The poor have had their wages raised, and better still, have been delivered from work relief and unemployment. They are self-supporting Americans again. Progressive income taxes are reducing the net incomes of the well to do. Where will the levels be when the war ends? Quincy Howe has estimated that no family will get much less than $2,500, or much more than $25,000—a ten-to-one range. It would take a long war, however, to reach this level.

The luxury trades will have been pretty well wiped out by D-Day, except such mass luxuries as movies, beer and cigarettes. Servants will be in the factories or fighting, and the women who stay at home will be doing most of their own work. Already the maid shortage parallels the gas shortage in Suburban Heights. Will servants who have found relative independence in the factory want to go back to "Yes, sir," "No, sir" and "Please, sir"?

Most powerful of all forces making for equality may be rationing. It will be directed more and more toward seeing that every American family receives the essentials of life. Mr. Byrnes has flatly said as much.[6] By D-Day there may be a graded distribution of essentials—the best cuts and qualities for the armed services, next best for the workers in heavy war industries, grade three for the rest of us, with Judy O'Grady doing just as well as the Colonel's lady.

A great steam roller is bearing down to flatten out economic classes and economic distinctions. The big house on the hill is closed, while the people across the tracks have more money than they can spend. It is not to be concluded, however, that we shall be reduced to one dead level of achievement. The steam roller promises to grind over stuffed shirts, deflating reputations blown up by fast-working publicity men. At the same time a new group of managers will be raised up, men who can get things done—produce goods, organize civilian effort, win battles, eliminate waste, bring us nearer to victory. The war on the home front still has its aspects of Hollywood, as *Life* once said. Sooner or later we have got to replace the stage men with real men.

New Patterns for Business

D-Day will see the structure of industry drastically revised. The so-called "concentration" movement may by then include many consumer goods industries. Take the manufacture of stoves. New stoves are now being produced in a few "nucleus" plants, primarily the more efficient factories. All

6. *The New York Times,* November 15, 1942.

other stove plants are converted or closed down for the duration, their labor distributed to war production. More than eighty consumer goods industries in Britain have been "concentrated," and we are beginning to follow the same road. The closed plants may keep a skeleton administrative staff; perhaps their brands will be kept alive by the nucleus plants. But in many cases, the private brands will be dropped in favor of "victory models," simplified and standardized stoves, shoes, household tools, furniture, and the rest.

Quite apart from the concentration program, it is inevitable that many thousands of small businesses should be eliminated as the war goes on. The vast roadside industry has already been hard hit—filling stations, garages, automobile and tire dealers, road houses. Many Main Street stores are being hit, and will be hit harder as the volume of consumers' goods declines. By the end of 1943, inventories are expected to be savagely reduced. The stores which remain in business will have to drop trimmings, frills and special services to the consumer. The customer will no longer always be right. The lady who orders five frocks expecting to return four of them after closer examination may get no service at all.

The whole great structure of competitive advertising no longer has much point. In Britain advertising is kept precariously alive by using space to advise the public *not to purchase* the advertiser's canned soup or his motor cars. In this country advertising still keeps going on "good will" campaigns, where the advertiser's name is tied up with "buy bonds now" and pictures of charging tanks. As the war strips us to bare essentials, one wonders how much of this can be retained. Salesmen are suffering a similar decline. Many are in the Army or in overalls.

Big business may be easier to recognize than little business when D-Day comes, but here also there are sure to be great changes. Many of the ablest executives are already working for the government, their horizons widened to a real comprehension of the public interest. Patent monopolies and prewar practices involving the restriction of output may be largely broken up. Some great industries—like the automobile industry already—will be working exclusively to government order when the war ends, producing not a single item for civilian use except possibly spare parts. It is not going to be easy to reconstruct the old techniques, where production was delicately adjusted to maximum profit or minimum loss. The market itself has disappeared for the duration.

Foreign trade in the old sense has already disappeared. Lend-lease now accounts for most of our exports, and such private traders as remain can move their goods only by permission of the Office of Economic Warfare. Perhaps we should drop the word "trade" for the duration. There are no free international markets left, almost no meeting of private buyers and sellers haggling for a just price. What we have now, and are sure to get more of, is a condition of exchange where the several governments decide what they will swap to speed the war effort, or to keep raw materials out of the hands of the Axis.

When the war ends, the economic systems of the United States, Britain, Canada, Mexico, the Caribbean countries, New Zealand, Australia, North Africa, may have been hammered into one super system which will make the old national tariffs, currencies, trade practices, look like remnants of the Stone Age. To unscramble this pattern will not be the work of a day.

The American crop output is sure to be very different on D-Day from what it was in 1941, being designed to feed armies and foreign allies as well as to provide subsistence for citizens on a balanced diet basis. There will be few surpluses dumped to rot. The farm labor force will be greatly changed. Perhaps squads of youngsters from the schools will do much of the seasonal work.

The railways, highways, airways, waterways, pipe lines, may be under one integrated control. This control, after the bugs are shaken out of it, may be so much more efficient in moving freight that one wonders how successful the effort will be to dismantle it.

The great American recreation industry, shorn of its cash customers by the restrictions on pleasure driving, may have retreated to its condition in about the year 1900.[7]

This is but a modest preview of the changed national picture on D-Day. If the war is long, the picture may be still more drastic. The date I had roughly in mind was early in 1946. Perhaps the end will come in two installments, the first in Europe, the second in the Far East. A military miracle or a sudden internal collapse of our enemies may happily move up the date of the final cease-firing order.

. . . The free market gone; foreign trade obliterated by lend-lease; the government ordering 60 to 70 per cent of everything produced; new and strange contractual relationships; the incentive of competition badly weakened; great areas of little business boarded up; a scarcity of man power, and the ranks of labor inundated by a flood from the middle class; the distribution of the national income leveled

7. See article by John R. Tunis, *Harper's*, May 1943.

and shifted in curious directions; the crop pattern rearranged; great taxes, great public debts, great levies of forced savings, great national income; the government in complete control of the banks; the British Empire and Latin America sitting in the middle of our laps. . . . Is there any road back?

One cannot operate a financial system in a vacuum. Behind the dollars lies a background of men, women and things. I have tried to indicate the surprising nature of that background on the day when the guns cease to speak.

3
POSTWAR GOALS

THERE MAY BE no road back from war economy, but there is a road forward. Its direction and destination are clear enough. We must find constructive work for most of those citizens now engaged in the destruction of our enemies. The returning soldiers, the disemployed workers in munitions plants, must have a place to go which offers them security and hope.

The New York Times is not noted for a revolutionary stand on economic questions, yet its leading editorial of December 9, 1942, put the case with no ifs, ands or buts:

Whatever obscurity may cloud other post-war goals, one goal is clear. All over the world masses of people have determined that the future world must be a world of full employment and production. It is not too much to say, as did the *Economist* of London recently, that this aspiration overrides all other political and social ideas.

Full employment may not be a categorical necessity on Monday morning after armistice, but it must be in the offing without unreasonable delay. It must be there to look forward to. People can be patient if they have hope. But any administration which fails to give them a well-justified hope, which shilly-shallies over the question, may presently find *itself* unemployed.

Plenty of Work to Be Done

Where is the constructive work to be found? We may look for it in four great categories:

1. In producing the essentials of food, shelter, clothing, medical care, education, so that every American family can be healthy and secure. Every family, almost without exception, will be getting the essentials on D-Day, but on a pretty Spartan basis. Now standards should rise to a decent living basis for all. The department of shelter will need immediate and drastic attention. Few permanent houses are being built during the war. Millions of workers may be living in barracks amid great congestion. Many will be quartered on private families, possibly by law. The private families may be thoroughly fed up. Housing constitutes probably the greatest single outlet for employment on the durable goods front when the war is over. To build 1,500,000 dwelling units a year—a minimum figure considering the accumulated shortage—would require roughly the labor of 2,000,000 workers.

2. In producing food and other essentials for countries beyond our borders. Europe will claim the most, but there will be many claims. North Africa is already heavily on the list. In an earlier book in this series, *Goals for America,* I estimated five million possible jobs in this division. As other nations get on their feet again, however, our shipments will be reduced, and the number of Americans employed in furnishing the supplies will fall. (I also allowed for another five million citizens continuing in the armed services and war industries. A huge policing or defense task will undoubtedly remain.)

3. In producing mass comforts for the people—automobiles, radios, washing machines, refrigerators, and other goods which the war has stricken from our budgets. There will also be a demand from the well to do for luxuries. A host of new products, made from plastics, glass, synthetics, light metals, are being developed by the war, and we shall want to try them out.

4. In reviving public works neglected during the war—schools, highways, hospitals and the like—and, if the employment gap is not filled, in new projects such as the reconstruction of cities to meet power age conditions, the integration of the continental transporta-

tion system, the development of other great rivers like the Tennessee.

Boys can go back to school, many women can go back to their homes, older men may retire, their war labors done. Perhaps this will take another five million off the labor front.

The four great categories listed above can be utilized to provide constructive work for all who still need employment, especially as the work week drops back to 40 hours.

Plenty of Skills

Meanwhile the labor force will not only be skilled beyond any other generation of Americans, but will have the last word in modern plant and machinery to assist it. The Defense Plant Corporation is now pouring $8 billions into new factories and equipment. Our output of electric energy is expected to be half again as great as in 1940, our machine tools to be increased threefold. Shipyards, mines, airfields, pipe lines, will be enormously expanded. True, the task of reconverting to peacetime goods will be great, but hardly greater than the task already accomplished in converting from peace to war.

There stand the workers, the tools and raw materials to work with, and the tasks to be done. The outlook from the physical standpoint is clear and hopeful. Unless the war lasts beyond limits not now imagined, we shall have all the physical requisites for building a great, expanding civilization in America, while helping the rest of the world to its feet.

We could achieve full employment and distribute the budget of necessities and comforts by a complete system of rationing, if there were no other way. Perhaps some items rationed under pressure of war—say milk for school children —will be kept on that basis. But rationing for a whole economy is a clumsy device, and demands totalitarian controls of the most drastic kind. The entire population becomes a disciplined army. Work and you will get your food and uniforms—maybe even cigarettes. Stop work and you go to the guardhouse. This may be good enough for Hitler, but it is not good enough for us. We shall have come close to it during the war, and we shall want no more of it.

Is Money Stronger?

Money is a far more flexible tool of distribution than rationing. It can also be a far more democratic tool, for it permits free choices in goods and in jobs. America will probably go on indefinitely using money for most purposes of distribution. We must try to employ it intelligently, for it is one of the most useful social inventions ever made. But, as in the case of mechanical inventions, we must be its master, not its slave.

Where is the money coming from to keep this fine physical structure in motion and so achieve the goals that we desire? Some people with whom I have discussed the matter throw up their hands. They do not believe that what the editors of the *Times* say must be done, can be done. They grant the strength of the physical structure, but declare that that isn't what counts. They say that the use of money is so charged with fear and emotion that we cannot have the physical things, because men will waste their efforts in fighting about who is to have the money. They point to the depression, when the physical structure did not in the least warrant the misery we endured. Like Mr. Berle's friends, they do not see how slums can be cleared without an earthquake, or a bombing.

Ah, a bombing! Is there any question that the slums of

London will be rebuilt as civilized housing after the war? None at all. Ask any Englishman. In war we are discovering that things which are physically possible are financially possible. We never had a total war before, and, as I tried to indicate in the last chapter, it is shaking our institutions to their foundations. What we did about all sorts of things, including money, before the war, forms no reliable pattern of what we can do, or will do, when the war is over. Money is slave, not master now; the lack of it does not halt the production of a single bomber.

When I grow discouraged about the passions men lavish on pieces of paper stamped with numbers, I repeat once and I repeat again, like Mr. Coué: *What is physically possible is financially possible.* Sooner or later, and perhaps as a direct result of total war, the world is going to believe this principle and act on it.

Learning from Stone Walls

I do not pretend to argue that because a thing ought to be done and can be done physically, it will be done. But I do believe that stone walls have a certain educational value. We have hit a lot of them already, and we are going to hit more. Closed minds are being knocked open. "You can't do that" is being replaced by "You can and must." Look at Mr. Kaiser's ships. Hope, vitality, confidence in our military and industrial ability, are in the air. There is a good fighting chance that this spirit will carry over into the peace.

In his budget message to Congress in January 1943, President Roosevelt called for $100 billions plus to be added to the $200 billions already appropriated for war. The total of more than $300 billions is greater than some estimates of the whole national wealth in 1932. The President indicated an annual Treasury deficit of $50 billions. This is greater than the total federal debt in 1939, a burden then believed by many citizens to be intolerable. Yet in one year of war we are going to swallow it up, and more.

We cannot stand in front of such figures as this, armed only with traditional concepts of sound finance. They indicate rates of spending, of debt, of deficit, as well as of production and national income, which have broken through the uttermost limits of what most Americans have hitherto believed possible.

The Old Yardsticks Are Broken

If we should try to use the old yardsticks, our hearts would freeze, our hands grow limp. How would it be possible to face, let alone handle, such stellar dimensions with orthodox ideas about annually balanced budgets, about national bankruptcy, about government spending as the road to ruin, rigorous economy as the road to prosperity, heavy taxation as an unmitigated evil, and all the other widely accepted concepts of 1940?

"We shall find," says Walter Lippmann, as he stands transfixed by the 1943 budget, "that in the presence of this demonstration of American productivity, the change of scale, the new order of magnitude of things, will compel us to re-examine all our common assumptions on such matters as taxes, the national debt, tariffs, international commerce, finance, imports, exports, and investments. . . . We have to find radically new premises from which to think about it at all."

Our enemies as well as our Allies show little sign of being

defeated by budgets relatively greater than our own. What have they learned that we have yet to learn?

Thinking on the old premises can lead only to despair. Fortunately there are new premises from which these vast spendings and debts can be judged. There is a way to look at them without being blinded by their immensity, and paralyzed by their implications. In the pages to follow we shall try to outline a financial scaffolding on which Americans can stand and look unflinchingly at one hundred billion dollar budgets.

To do it we shall have to go back to first principles for a bit and get a good grasp on certain facts about the nature and behavior of money.

4

THE POTATO MODEL

Whⁿen an airplane designer wants to know how a given plane will work, he makes a model and puts it in a wind tunnel. He varies the wind pressure and sees what happens to his ship.

A great money system is a product of complex factors, hard to measure in action. Many models have been constructed to illustrate it—the favorite locus being Robinson Crusoe's island. Of all the models I have seen, including a few I have built myself, I prefer that of a Minnesota banker, which has become a classic in the last few years. Its performance in the wind tunnel is significant. It is simple to understand, some may say too simple. True, it does neglect many major characteristics of the big reality, and we must use it with caution. It shows, however, how dollars flow around the money circuit, and exactly how the flow can be broken and repaired again. Arthur Dahlberg calls it "basic and vital to an understanding of all recovery plans related to the monetary mechanism."[1]

The designer of the model is Ralph Manuel, president of

1. *Recovery Plans,* Temporary National Economic Committee, Monograph No. 25, 1940. Mr. Dahlberg describes Mr. Manuel's model at length, quoting his earlier testimony before the TNEC.

the Marquette National Bank of Minneapolis. He asks us to consider a small community where people produce and consume nothing but potatoes. Monotonous, if you like, but easy to grasp. They appoint a managing committee which gives out claim checks for work in the potato fields—a check for a day's work, or a week's work, or what you will. After the harvest is in, it is found that there are, say, 4,000 bushels in the warehouse and that 2,000 claim checks have been distributed. Thus each check is good for two bushels of potatoes. (Any combination of figures can be used. If it were 2,000 bushels and 4,000 claim checks, then each check would be good for half a bushel.) The members of the community line up, present their claim checks and haul away their share.

Here we have an economy where the money is claim checks, and where perfect balance is maintained between goods and money. It can never suffer from unemployment, booms or depressions. It can only suffer from droughts, plagues and frosts—genuine disasters. The money flows out to the producers, the goods flow in to the warehouse; then the money flows in to the warehouse, and the potatoes flow out to the producer-consumers. Finally the claim checks are torn up. Everything is under control. This is the money circuit in its simplest form.

When Claim Checks Are Saved

But suppose, continues our banker, that the claim checks are *not* torn up but used over and over again. Now the door is open for trouble. Some members of the community decide to *save* some of their claim checks against a future harvest. They hide the checks under the hearthstone and take less from the warehouse. The potatoes represented by their hidden checks are not claimed. They stand in the warehouse and presently spoil.

Next season the managers arrange for a smaller crop. This means less employment for all or total unemployment for some. It also means less to eat. Our little economy is sliding into a depression. If there is any more saving, it will get worse. Presently things may become so bad that the people will say to hell with it, throw out the claim check system, and go back to barter.

When members of the potato community want to save their claim checks, there is just one way to do it without wrecking the system. *They must give the checks, or loan them, to somebody else to take to the warehouse.* In that way all the current claim checks get back to clear the current crop.

Now let us speculate about the savers a little more. We can use the potato model to indicate roughly the processes of investment. Suppose the savers are not just foolish hoarders, but men with imagination, who see a way to increase the output of potatoes, and so benefit the whole community. They reduce their own consumption of potatoes and give what they save to other workers. These workers are asked to stop hoeing potatoes and go to work making wheelbarrows. This the workers do, meanwhile living on the extra potatoes they have been given.

Next season, with wheelbarrows on hand, the community can produce more potatoes per man-hour. The savers have proved themselves to be beneficent investors. Why should they not get their claim checks back, plus a bit more for the good they have done? The community can afford it, for it now has a larger crop. The savers, by turning into investors, have made progress possible.

Claim Checks for Newcomers

Let us put the model through one last maneuver. Suppose a group of strangers comes over the hill. They have only a small supply of food and no claim checks. No member of the community has claim checks he can afford to give them. In brief, there is no money. So the outlanders must starve? Not at all, say the managers. Here are the fields. Go to work like the rest of us, and we will give you claim checks as you produce. We can afford the money if you can afford the work. Thus the community expands its production and its money supply simultaneously. Observe, however, that if the managers had just handed out new claim checks to the strangers for nothing, they could have cut in on the potatoes and reduced the share of all the regular workers. This may be charity, but hardly justice.

In more complicated communities, where people are puzzled about the performance of money, it is often held that unemployed or destitute people cannot be put to work because the community cannot afford it. Where is the money to come from? If they had studied Mr. Manuel's model they would not ask this question. It would be apparent that if facilities are available, any new production is warrant for new claim checks.

This potato model illustrates three fundamental characteristics of the money mechanism. First, that claim checks paid out during the course of production must come back to the warehouse if the crop is to be cleared. Second, that claim checks can be saved without breaking the circuit, provided the savers transfer them to somebody else to take to the warehouse. If the transfer encourages the production of wheelbarrows or other improved tools, the savers become helpful investors, aiding progress. Third, a community can afford to distribute more claim checks in return for more production. Not money but work is the deciding factor.

The Big Community

Now let us widen the model to the dimensions of the whole American economy, but still keeping it pretty simple. Suppose that in the course of a year businessmen and other agents of production pay out 100 billion dollars in wages, salaries, interest, profits.[2] The whole amount represents the cost of goods and services produced during the year, plus the profit expected from them. The whole amount lands in the collective pocket of the nation. So if the nation lines up at the counter prepared to spend 100 billion dollars for goods and services, the year's production will be cleared at the prices asked. Of course competitive conditions may cause some producers to lose out, but others will gain, and the economy as a whole will continue on an even keel.

But suppose, as is often the case, that the nation saves 20 per cent of its income. If it is all hoarded, only 80 billion dollars will come back on the market. There is a yawning gap of 20 billions in the circuit. The agents of production are in a pretty fix. Their prices fall headlong, inventories pile up on the shelves, crops are left to rot or are deliberately destroyed, workers are turned out on the streets. Banks call their loans in a hurry.

If the savings are invested, however, not in speculative run-arounds but in job-producing enterprises, then the 20

2. When the economy as a whole is considered, the money paid out for *materials* becomes somebody else's income, and *he* pays it out in wages, salaries, interest and profit. Materials have no use for money, and it all lands up in some person's pocket.

billions get back on the market and the gap is closed. But the action must be prompt. The gap opens not only because of hoarded money, but because of money destined for investment which creeps slowly along frozen channels.

It is the *rate* which counts. The rate of spending must equal the rate of production. ($100 billions each, in the model.) The rate of spending in turn is composed of the rate of direct spending ($80 billions), and the rate of investment ($20 billions). Obviously if the investment rate is only half the savings rate, then a 10 billion dollar gap opens. It must be offset somehow, or a depression will surely develop, and the economy will go on part time.

Where Economists Agree

It has been said that if you laid all the economists end to end they would never reach an agreement. The wisecrack has merit, but there is at least one exception to it. Economists will agree, almost to a man, on the potato principle. They will affirm that the money paid out in the course of producing goods, whether it be potatoes, thumb tacks or locomotives, is substantially enough to buy the product back. The National Resources Planning Board phrases it in this way:

Full employment cannot be maintained unless there is returned to the income stream in each period all that is paid out in the previous period. Whatever individuals and corporations wish to save out of full employment levels must necessarily be offset by net investment expenditures. . . .[3]

The Brookings Institution at Washington reinforces the statement:

Inadequacy of consumptive demand is not . . . attributable to the

3. *War Time Planning for Continuing Full Employment*, NRPB Report, August 1942.

alleged fact that market prices of commodities necessarily exceed the sums disbursed in connection with their production. The truth is that there is an identity between the market price of a commodity and the sums received by those who have engaged in its production. If $100 is paid for a commodity, $100 is received by the seller, and any difference accruing to him over and above the disbursements to others for materials, interest, wages, etc., is profit. Since profits are also available for expenditure, they must obviously be included in the picture; and when included, selling prices and the income of producers necessarily must be equal. . . .

The failure of consumptive demand to equal in magnitude the volume of goods that might have been produced is attributable . . . to the fact that a substantial portion of the income was not expended for consumption goods but was diverted to savings channels, where much of it failed to be used productively.[4]

So long as our dollars come back to the market at about the same rate we receive them, the national economy remains in balance—assuming that costs and prices remain reasonably stable. If they vary too widely, of course, the flow of goods and dollars will be distorted or interrupted, just as the distribution of potatoes would be interfered with if their price in claim checks were arbitrarily changed. It is important that the dollar circuit be kept free from stoppages of this kind too.

Unlike the potato community, our great system has no tidy season of production followed by a season of distribution. In our big community the seasons overlap. It may take only a few weeks to complete the circuit in eggs, and several years to complete it for a giant turbine. The process is dynamic, with production and selling going on together. A given year intersects the process at both ends, with many cycles incomplete. There is no way to halt the economy in motion and

4. Harold G. Moulton, *The Formation of Capital*, Brookings Institution, 1935.

look at it carefully. That is why the potato model is helpful. It halts one process and gives us an indication of the rhythms of them all.

But if we never saved our money progress would be impossible. There would be no claim checks for new wheelbarrows or better mousetraps. There would be no capital for investment, no debts, no interest, no bonds, stocks or mortgages. There would be nothing to be called "capitalism." The whole output would be consumers' goods. Profits would not be invested but would be spent for consumers' goods as fast as they were produced. This would constitute a 100 per cent consumption economy, the normal pattern of mankind for thousands of years, and of many primitive peoples today. There is no progress and there is no unemployment.

In recent years we have had great sums in the form of savings set aside for progress, but because they were not promptly invested we have had terrible unemployment. Part of our trouble has been that one set of people make the decisions about savings, and another set make the decisions about investment, and their incentives are different. Those who make investment decisions are naturally more cautious and temperamental than the savers, with the result that the rate of saving tends to be steadier than the rate of investment.

Somewhere between the extremes of a 100 per cent consumption economy, and an economy which saves too much, the balance must lie. What we want is a community in which savings flow into investment channels in a steady enough stream and in sufficient volume to employ all our people and to keep the dollar circuit closed.

5

NUMBERS WHICH MOVE

No community in the world has ever had a money system as simple as Mr. Manuel's potato economy. Even a barter system is more complicated, and when barter gave way to the use of some sort of currency, people had to learn its use. Money has always been a manmade bundle of conventions, rules and taboos. Children have to be taught how to behave about money, much as they are taught how to behave about going to church.

Until recent years, money has also been a physical thing, valuable in itself. This physical currency has varied from cattle (Latin *pecus,* hence *pecuniary*) to slaves, wampum, mats, furs, coconuts, rice, the great stone wheels of Yap, copper, iron, bronze, silver and gold. Thus, to complete any exchange, three physical things were involved. You swapped, say, maize for wampum; then at your convenience you swapped the wampum for a bow and arrow. When straight barter becomes too slow and clumsy, men have always turned to money. It is a social invention which can speed up transfers and so help produce more goods. But as long as the currency in itself had value, the exchange could stop in the middle, so to speak, leaving the seller with his cows or furs or decorative wampum.

During the last century, and especially since the last war, the wampum quality has been fading out of money. Today in 1943, every civilized nation has virtually dropped its wampum. Citizens swap physical things for pieces of paper with numbers stamped upon them. The paper is valueless. For small change, token coins are stamped with numbers, but they have little value as metal. Some coins are already going synthetic. Wooden nickels on a plywood plastic formula would be quite satisfactory if they carried the stamp, and would fit the slot machines. "Fiat currency" has long been a term of reproach for money which had no solid metal behind it. Today the whole world deals in fiat currency—paper stamped with numbers. Its validity rests on production, output, labor, machine-hours.

A Little Experiment

When I was first told that money was numbers it sounded like nonsense to me. The gold reflex was deep in my cerebellum. But I was willing to learn. So I left the endless talk about money, and proceeded to observe what I did with it in a year's time. I shut my mouth and looked at my hands. I imitated what the physicists call the operational approach. Instead of using words when they want to define a theory, physicists perform an operation in the laboratory. The definition comes out of what they do.[1]

I found that all I received during the year from my various labors came in the form of pieces of paper with numbers written or stamped on them: "Pay to the order of Stuart Chase . . . $100." I found almost all I paid out during the year was in precisely the same form: "Pay to the order of

1. See P. W. Bridgman, *The Logic of Modern Physics*, Macmillan, 1927.

Sears, Roebuck . . . $18.51." In addition I handed out some pieces of paper with numbers engraved on them by the government, and some small coins with numbers stamped on them. I got the currency by swapping a check for it, of the same number: "Pay to the order of Cash . . . $10."

At first I thought the checks themselves were money, but strictly speaking I found they are not. They are orders to pay money. The money itself is numbers on a ledger in a bank. This can readily be demonstrated by the fact that losing a check is not disastrous, but receiving a "no funds" statement is. The fighting numbers are in your account; the check is only an order on the bank to release them. If checks were money, we could all get blank checkbooks and go to town.

I handled no gold during that year, nothing solid at all except the aforesaid small stamped coins. All my income came in the form of checks and my outgo went in the same form, except that perhaps 10 per cent of the outgo was in the shape of pocket currency. Thus I dealt in bank money almost altogether; currency was a minor matter. When the numbers in my bank account were relatively high—as per the monthly statement—I felt good. When they were low, I felt terrible.

Having performed this little experiment, I never expect to handle a gold piece—or a negotiable cow—as long as I live. Why should I? The numbers exchange for whatever I want and can afford, and a cow would mess up my study. A little looking about me, still with my mouth shut and the textbooks closed, made it clear that my behavior was typical of everybody in the country, including corporations. Wage earners deal more in paper currency and less in checks—but both are numbers on paper. Every man jack of us is swapping things for numbers, and numbers for things. More than 90 per cent of all exchanges in the country in a normal year's time are made by check.

Traveling in Mexico, I used to go around loaded down with silver pesos, like a commando loaded down with lethal hardware. It was a relief to get back to the States and load up with a checkbook. The sheer inconvenience of hard money would doom it if any more convenient system could be found.

Good as Gold

Gold still has some medicinal value as a fortifier of confidence. Many elderly people feel easier knowing that it is there in a vault somewhere. But every nation has abandoned the gold standard internally, while lend-lease has made it superfluous in settling most balances between nations. When the United States left gold in 1933, the dollar was supposed to be worth 59 cents forthwith, but the internal price level hardly quivered. Five cent cigars still sold for a nickel. Many authorities believe that gold had lost its function as active money long before the recent flight from the gold standard. Says E. H. Carr, for instance:[2]

The international gold standard currency of the nineteenth century was, like all other currencies, a "managed" currency. Thanks to the supremacy of the London money market, which financed a considerable proportion of international trade, and was a frequent and lavish lender to overseas countries, this international currency was "managed" by the bankers and bill-brokers of London. The gold standard was the symbol and the instrument of British financial hegemony; it was, in fact, just as much a sterling as a gold standard.

Arthur Dahlberg traces the following historical sequence:[3]

1. Gold was adopted as active money and passed from hand to hand in buying and selling goods.

2. *Conditions of Peace,* Macmillan, 1942.   3. TNEC Monograph No. 25.

2. Warehouse receipts were substituted for gold, being easier to carry around; but gold to the full value of the receipts was held in the banker's vaults.

3. Gold certificates displaced the warehouse receipts. Bankers found that as the gold itself was not often demanded, they could issue certificates, and so make loans, *against more gold than they had in their vaults.*

This happened long ago in the countinghouses of Europe, *but it was the beginning of modern credit money.* The total money which people used ceased to be backed by an equal amount of gold. A part of it was pure numbers on paper. That part has been growing ever since, until now the physical thing has all but disappeared, and been supplanted by paper money "managed" by bankers or by the state. Awareness of this fact, says David C. Coyle, "will prevent undue astonishment when the money of a nation appears and disappears like a scene in a movie."[4]

The United States abandoned the gold standard in 1933, but did not quite abandon gold. After 1933, no American could get gold to use as money; he had to take paper, and not even gold certificates at that. People who expected the world to end were surprised. They did not realize how far numbers money had already displaced hard money. The Treasury continued to buy gold from abroad, and from mining companies, for 35 paper dollars per ounce, and buried it in Fort Knox. The effect of this policy was to give foreigners and mining companies the wherewithal to buy American goods in exchange for nothing useful. It can be defended on similar grounds to lend-lease. The Treasury's gold still acts as a theoretical brake on the amount of new money the banks can create, but as the Treasury now has most of the

4. David Cushman Coyle, *Roads to a New America,* Little, Brown, 1938.

gold in the world the brake is only a figure of speech.

Where Does New Money Come From?

As matters stand today, what I use as money, you use as money, the nation uses as money, consists of:

1. Demand deposits in banks, subject to check.
2. Currency—paper dollars and stamped metal coins.

The total stock of money can be increased in four ways:

1. By the banks' making new loans to commercial enterprises—in excess of loans retired.
2. By the banks' making loans to the government in exchange for government bonds.
3. By the government's creating new dollars through bonds deposited in its own central bank—the Federal Reserve, in our case.
4. By the government's printing new currency.

How does a bank create new money? You go to your bank with a proposition for $10,000. It is accepted. The bank takes your note for $10,000, and puts it in the safe. You are then given a deposit account of $10,000 on the bank's ledgers—less the bank's discount or profit. You are given a checkbook, and told to go to it. You can draw checks up to the full amount of the account, and they are accepted in all monetary transactions.

When the time comes to pay off your note, you may do it by drawing a check to the order of the bank on your account in the bank. Whereupon, presto! $10,000 disappears from the total money in the national system.

Observe that the bank has created no new currency, or money in the sense of legal tender, but it has brought new numbers into the system. Your proposition for $10,000 was presumably for the creation of new wealth—corn you proposed to plant, or shoes you proposed to manufacture. The numbers, accordingly, were not issued against nothing. Wealth to be produced in the future was "monetized." You can call it an extension of credit if you wish, but the fact remains that you can spend that credit by drawing checks on a new deposit account.

A similar thing happens when the government sells a $10,000 war bond to the bank. Uncle Sam gets a new deposit account forthwith, and can draw checks up to $10,000—less the discount. This is happening now on a tremendous scale. New numbers are being pumped into the system so fast that the country is in terror of inflation. We shall examine this point further in Chapter 9.

The Number of Dollars in the System

On any given day there are exactly so many dollars in the system. In early 1943, there were about 60 billion units in bank deposits subject to check, and 15 billion units in pants' pockets, purses and tills—75 billion altogether. The Treasury statement for November 30, 1942, showed the following currency in circulation:

Federal Reserve notes ("bills" of various denominations)	$11,667,000,000
Silver certificates	1,731,000,000
Coins	793,000,000
Other currency ("bills" of various kinds and denominations)	614,000,000
Total currency	$14,805,000,000

Thus most of our currency is in the form of Federal Reserve notes—the usual dollar or five-dollar bills. There was $22,-743,000,000 of gold in the Treasury as of November 30, 1942, but it was not counted as money, and properly so.

In 1929 there were only some 31 billion units in the system as against 75 in 1943, and unemployment was at a minimum. In 1939 there were 45 billion units in the system, but almost 10 million persons were unemployed. *These figures reduce to nonsense proposals for always bringing prosperity by pumping more dollars into the system.* With 14 billion fewer dollars in 1929 than in 1939 we had practically full employment.

What is the answer? The answer is that the 1929 dollars were *moving, working,* while many of the 1939 dollars were idle, unemployed. If men are to work, dollars must work too, in the sense of traveling briskly around the circuit. In the potato community, when claim checks were hoarded, the crop was not cleared and unemployment began.

I am not trying to instruct you in the detailed workings of the banking system. They are highly technical and beyond the scope of this book.[5] I am trying to make just two points: first, that the banks, under the rules of the Federal Reserve, have the power to create and to cancel money; second, that the place of gold in controlling that creation is now pretty nebulous. In some countries it is completely absent.

The total number of dollars in the system is a figure of some importance, but far more important is the *rate at which dollars are exchanged for things,* as we noted in the last chapter. One hundred dollars in my pocket, or in my bank account, may make me feel good, but it is of no material value to me until it is exchanged. I cannot eat it, wear it, admire its glitter, any more than I can a page of algebra. Modern money is not wealth but a ticket which may be exchanged for wealth—now, or at some future date. If prices

5. For a clear description of the complicated process of creating bank money, see John Philip Wernette, *Money, Business and Prices,* 1933.

change in the future, then the wealth I can claim will be different from what I can claim now. If prices should go up out of sight, I could claim practically nothing. The fear of inflation lies in this possibility.

A Store of Value

It should be pointed out here that money has another characteristic than the one emphasized in this chapter; namely, it constitutes a "store of value." While modern money is no longer valuable in itself, it does give the holder a claim on goods in the future, and unless inflation intervenes, this claim does not depreciate. If you should store butter for future claims on other goods, it would depreciate very rapidly. Most fabricated things depreciate to some degree, although some, like Old Masters and rare postage stamps, go up in value. But money tends to remain at par. People realize this in their behavior when they try to keep a considerable fraction of their property in cash.

No Production, No Money

Suppose everybody in the country has $5,000 in the bank. So everybody decides to call it a day and take it easy. But after the store shelves are cleared out, the money soon becomes useless as buying power. With nobody working, nothing is brought to market. Production having stopped, money stops too. No production, no money. What good are claim checks if there are no potatoes? This is the extreme case of money which does not move, but it serves to show that modern money receives its credentials primarily from labor and production. No community can get rich, except by the work of men and machines.

We all know this. The trouble is that we do not always act as if we knew it. When a depression threatens, many of us try to convert securities and other assets into cash. This stops the flow of money into goods and makes the depression worse. Obviously the more liquid we get, the more slowly money moves, the more workers lose their jobs, the fewer goods are produced.[6]

Hard Money Cuts Deep

Money now is numbers. You swap your wheat crop for some numbers and then you turn around and swap the numbers for a new piano. Everybody uses numbers, but not everybody knows in his mind what his hands are doing. Gold has cut deeply into human consciousness and the marks are still there. Many of us think of money as something glittering, durable, valuable in itself, though the money we use burns like autumn leaves. We think of money as an entity, as a fixed fund—in the sense that what one man gains another must lose.

Even when Congress appropriates ten times more money for a couple of years of war than the dollar value of all the gold mined since the Java Man, people still cling to the hard money concept. That is why they ask: "Where's the money coming from?" They find it difficult to grasp the newer concepts, where money is dynamic, like an electric current, not static like a ton of pig iron; where the numbers are really based not on gold but on production. There is no untested theory in this statement. It is a cold description of what the money managers of every belligerent nation are now doing.

6. Bassett Jones, an engineer who used the operational test for money, has defined it as "a rate of transfer of numbers." That is, without movement of the numbers, money ceases to mean much of anything.

If they did not do it, they would lose the war in very short order by limiting production to the hard money available.

Whether the numbers are tied to gold or not is unimportant so long as the gold does not cripple their movement. John Maynard Keynes and the U.S. Treasury have recently released tentative plans for a postwar world bank, or clearinghouse, which would use some gold in settling balances between nations. The prospects for employing the gold standard internally by any nation after the war look remote.

The science of managing money as numbers is now being forged in the furnace of war, and great progress is being made, as we shall see. The techniques are often complicated, but the principles are simple. Let us repeat them again:

Keep the dollars moving. Get the claim checks back to the warehouse.

Never pump new dollars into the system faster than goods are being produced. If you do, the excess of dollars will force up the price of goods and the spiral of inflation will begin.

6

THE DOLLAR CIRCUIT

Now that we have tried to shed some light on the nature and behavior of money, let us go back and look more closely at the subject of savings and investment. If savings are not promptly invested in productive work, trouble begins. This is, I believe, the most important trouble to be found in the modern financial world.

The Brookings Analysis

The Brookings Institution at Washington has studied this dilemma in a series of four excellent books,[1] and we will follow their analysis part of the way.

Savings, the Brookings Institution finds, were large during the 1920's. The distribution of the national income was such that the well to do were quite unable, as a class, to spend their whole income on consumers' goods and were forced to save a large amount. Of the $15 billions of savings estimated for 1929, $13 billions belonged to 10 per cent of the population. *Sixty thousand* families with high incomes saved as

1. See its publications: *America's Capacity to Produce*, 1934; *America's Capacity to Consume*, 1934; *Formation of Capital*, 1935; *Income and Economic Progress*, 1935. These four titles have also been issued in one volume, *Distribution of Income in Relation to Economic Progress*, 1936.

much as *25 million* families with low incomes. People with incomes of $10,000 and over accounted for two thirds of the whole savings fund. There was a progressive increase of such persons from 1900 to 1929. It meant that opportunities for productive investment had to increase as fast as the savings, or idle capital would result.

Orthodox economists, say the Brookings authors, have never worried about this situation. They have argued that if income were not spent directly it would be promptly reinvested, and so returned to the income stream.[2] This theory seems to have grown up while the world was chronically short of capital in the eighteenth and nineteenth centuries, a period when four great continents were being developed. The economists got used to the rhythm and expected it to continue indefinitely. Savings, they thought, would always automatically find productive investment.

The demand for consumers' goods, and the investment of savings in the new plant, were thought to be independent of one another. Plants would be built, capital would find productive outlets, even if consumer demand were declining.

No! says the Brookings Institution, and proceeds methodically to prove its case. The statistical record shows that new plants are built chiefly *when consumer demand is increasing.* This not only is statistically proved but it makes sense. Why run up a new shoe factory if the demand for shoes is falling off? The two curves are not independent, as the orthodox economists believed, but *firmly linked.* New shoe factories

2. Arthur Dahlberg, in TNEC Monograph No. 25 referred to above, explains their attitude by quoting Say's "law" about the dollar circuit. The law held that over-all demand for goods always equaled the supply of goods and, except for temporary ups and downs, *stability automatically prevailed.* The orthodox, relying on Say's "law," have never faced the fact of a chronic decline in demand, due to excess savings.

are a function of the demand for shoes; their curves go up and down together.

It may be objected that when consumers spend briskly they do not save so much, and thus capital for new shoe factories is hard to find. This is a logical objection. If people are taking all their claim checks to the warehouse for potatoes, where is the money for wheelbarrows to come from? There would be none available in the potato community. But in our greater community, there are ways to get it, as Brookings points out and as every banker knows.

If a community uses only gold for active money, the sole way to introduce more money into the system is to dig or import more gold. Not so with modern credit money, as we have seen. New numbers can be created by the banks—up to the limit imposed by their "reserves." Bank credit makes it possible to spend more, save more, reinvest more. This extreme flexibility is both an asset and a danger.

New plants, then, are dependent on the demand for consumers' goods. But, according to the Brookings studies, new plants have no direct statistical relation to the volume of savings. From 1922 to 1929 savings showed an increase year by year, but plant investment in private enterprise did not increase at the same rate. In 1929, of total savings of $15 billions only $5 billions were so invested. In nearly every line of activity, plant capacity during the twenties exceeded market demand. Even in that boom year of 1929, capacity was estimated at 19 per cent above demand, for the plant as a whole.

Our capacity to produce consumer goods has been chronically in excess of the amount which consumers are able, or willing, to take off the markets; and this situation is attributable to the increasing proportion of the total income which is diverted to savings channels. The result is a chronic inability—despite such devices as high pressure salesmanship, installment credits and loans to facilitate foreign purchases—to find market outlets adequate to absorb our full productive capacity.[3]

So much for the Brookings analysis. Now we return to Chase.

One Dollar Out of Five

In a comparatively normal year, the American people, including corporations, save about one dollar out of five. They put it in savings banks, regular banks, life insurance premiums, building and loan associations; into stocks, bonds, mortgages and depreciation reserves. Sometimes they put it under the mattress, but usually straight hoarding does not amount to much. In 1932, however, people were putting currency, and even gold, into safe deposit boxes—more reliable than mattresses, but with precisely the same disastrous effect on the dollar circuit. When there was a crying need that money should move, people did their best to freeze it.

If most savings in normal times go to the banks and other institutions, why is not that an investment? Because the institutions may not think there is a good opportunity to invest your money. Their cash piles up, and their rate of investment is cautious and slow. Mr. Manuel tells of a businessman who had $85,000 on deposit in his bank during most of the depression. The numbers sat there doing nothing. The savings banks and insurance companies have been stuffed with uninvested cash for years. Now they are stuffed with war bonds, and the cash has gone into war factories and pay rolls.

The Lag in Investment

Why have investments declined relative to savings? The

3. *Income and Economic Progress,* p. 46.

economists laid end to end certainly do not agree on the answer to this one. Among the various explanations which they advance, the following make the most sense to me:

The leveling curve of population, with its leveling effect on real estate values, among other things.

The end of continental expansion in the United States.

The collapse of foreign investments, beginning in 1928 and 1929.

The increasing efficiency of a dollar of new plant investment today over what it used to be.

Greater caution among investors when government policies alarm them. The individual saver hesitates to take a chance, and keeps his money in the bank.

A series of pendulum swings during one phase of which investments overreach our needs while in the other they fall short.

So long as we use money as an economic tool, we must respect its limitations. It cannot do everything. It is a tool for distributing potatoes and other goods. Its smooth operation has little to do with the justice of the distribution, but depends directly on having all the goods distributed to someone, so that the circuit is completed.

Dated Money

Theoretically the claim checks should be canceled after the current crop is cleared. If money had no purchasing power after a given date, we should fall over ourselves to spend it or invest it while it was still good. Professor Irving Fisher and others have drafted plans for dated money. It would work splendidly in the potato economy, but I am not so sure about our own. There is no date when all production is completed and the cycle begins again. A thousand kinds of production are all operating simultaneously in different time cycles. It would do no good to date currency unless bank money were dated too—and where is a reliable method for doing that?

If Professor Fisher or somebody *could* devise a workable scheme, and if it were adopted, I venture to say that most of the mystery and confusion about money would disappear. People never get hot and bothered about railroad tickets. The ticket is good from Chicago to St. Louis, and no farther. The conductor punches it, clippity-clip, and that is the end of it. Similarly, with a dated money system, the dollar created by somebody's contribution to the general pot of production would go to buy back one dollar's worth of that production, whereupon, clippity-clip, its task is done. There would be scarcely a money crank left in the country after a year or two of this. Even William Jennings Bryan could have kept his shirt on, had dated money been in force.

If the proposal is too difficult to introduce, then we need to use our more or less timeless numbers in ways which give substantially the same effect—get them back into the market before the potatoes begin to rot.

Printing Press Money

There is an artificial way which we have already mentioned to close the gap between demand and goods, but it is a dangerous one. That is for the government to print dollars and give them to people to spend.[4] This clears the potatoes all right, but shoots a stream of new claim checks into the system for which no potatoes have been produced. There is no work, no wealth, back of such numbers.

It is at this point that sober citizens protest most vigorously against "government spending," and with good reason. A government which makes a practice of printing money to

4. Printing bonds and giving them to the banks, who then create bank money for the government to draw on, has a similar effect.

offset savings is bound to land in a runaway inflation. The system gets so loaded with numbers that it finally explodes. Then the community may have to begin all over again with a new kind of claim check, as Germany did in 1924, when the old mark was replaced by the Reichsmark. It is not the end of the community by any means—witness Germany—but it is ferociously hard on many citizens, especially those with fixed salaries and incomes.

Criticism should be leveled at a particular kind of government spending, not at all government spending as such. There has been too much of the latter kind—indiscriminate criticism based on fear and ignorance. The men in government, after all, are responsible for keeping the community afloat. A point comes where they are obliged to take steps to clear the potatoes—steps that nobody else is willing or able to take. Businessmen certainly cannot do this job in a depression.

The government does not necessarily have to print money. Instead it can go after the frozen money already in the system. If it taxes idle savings back into the stream of spending, there is no creation of new dollars, no increase in debt, no danger of inflation. There will be squawks from the savers, but the dollar circuit can thus be closed. This problem is vital today in financing the war. The more old numbers the government can collect through taxes, the fewer new numbers it will need to borrow from the banks.

Again, if the government prints money and gives it to workers for producing, say, a Boulder Dam, the danger is reduced, for the new dollars are backed with new wealth, just as they are when new bank money is spent for private construction. If the procedure is financed by borrowing old numbers from savers there is no danger of inflation at all. If it is financed by new money which later can be retired, as full employment and high levels of national income are reached, the risk may be justified by the probable gain. Only if the public works projects are useless in generating future activity, while forcing the national debt up year after year, can the procedure be condemned out of hand. Dams, highways, schools, hospitals and the like, open new opportunities for permanent employment and new opportunities for private investment. Look at the roadside industries which used to spring up along a fine new highway—and will again.

Can We Trust the Managers?

It may be objected that you cannot trust the men in charge of the government. But who else is there to trust? What other agency has the power to close the circuit when savers will not invest? There is no other agency. The argument that the government is too corrupt or incompetent to do it is a counsel of despair. It means that we must surrender helplessly to the financial conventions we have created.

Peter F. Drucker believes that during the past ten years the knowledge and understanding of money have made greater strides than any other branch of the social sciences.[5] He cites the techniques of the Exchange Equalization Fund in international finance, and those of government "deficit spending" in internal finance. This knowledge, be it observed, has come in as we have learned that the internal price level can be kept stable when currency is released from gold.

Summary of the Dollar Circuit

Let us gather up the threads of the last three chapters.

5. *Harper's*, May 1941.

1. Modern money is not a physical entity but the transfer of numbers according to a set of rules. The numbers are in bank ledgers or stamped on bills and coins. Their connection with gold is remote.

2. The numbers must move from hand to hand, encouraging production and employment, to be of use.

3. The act of production always releases enough numbers to buy the product back, and thus to keep the economy in balance.

4. But the money must be spent, either directly, or via the investment route. If it is not spent, a gap will appear in the circuit and unemployment will begin.

5. The gap can be closed by printing new money, by taxing old money back into the spending stream, or by borrowing. Either printing or borrowing is dangerous unless new production is behind it. Either can stuff the system with dollars until it blows up in a runaway inflation.

6. As a community grows, new money is needed from time to time, even when no gaps appear in the circuit. The banks have the power to supply it by crediting a borrower's account with the amount of his note. They can also reduce the numbers in the system by reversing the machinery—calling their loans.

7. When people think of money as gold or silver, they find it hard to see that the unemployed can be put to work. They think of a fixed sum, which, if shared with the unemployed, would impoverish the rest of the community. But modern money is not a fixed sum. It is so dynamic and flexible that it can always be expanded to finance new work or new production if there is any slack in the economy at all. Far from being impoverished, everyone gains when employment goes

up—gains to the extent of the new wealth created by those hitherto unemployed.

8. An economy on part time should follow different rules from an economy on full time. When everyone has a job, the dollar circuit is functioning satisfactorily and it is unwise to monkey with it. But severe and chronic unemployment is prima-facie evidence that the circuit is broken. Energetic and specific steps must then be taken to close it or the whole financial mechanism will presently fall apart—as it did when the American banks shut their doors in 1933. Never again can a modern state afford to wait, as we waited from 1929 to 1933, for some unknown god from some machine to come and save us.

7

THE CIRCUIT ROLLS

IN THIS CHAPTER and the next we shall attempt to trace the performance of the dollar circuit in America over the past century, with special attention to the way the principles we have studied earlier worked out in practice. We shall not try to write economic history so much as we shall look for breaks in the circuit and observe how they were filled.

It is hoped that the reader will get from these chapters a sense of the actual forces which generate prosperity or depression. Equipped with this sense, he may be better able to understand the grave problems which will follow D-Day.

The Rhythm of a Century

The numbers were rolling smoothly around the dollar circuit in 1913. To a young man fresh from Harvard—such a young man as I pictured in *The Road We Are Traveling*—money and business looked sound and serene. There had been no serious price inflation since the Civil War, and the gold standard ranked with home and mother in the national affections.

After 1820 . . . the spectacular growth of American population guaranteed constantly expanding markets. The great burst of turn-pike, canal and railroad building promised to make those markets accessible at every season of the year. The high rate of profit for successful firms drew more and more capitalists into factory enter-prises and made it easier to finance rapid plant expansion.[1]

For a century the dollar circuit had been expanding. It would slow down from time to time as a result of excessive speculation, but it always got under way again. In a rough and general way, the American economy followed this rhythm:

Savings were invested in new plant and equipment, providing employment for construction workers.

The new plant employed more people and turned out more goods.

The greater flow of goods raised standards of living, increased the national income, and made more savings possible.

The additional savings were again invested.

Toward the close of the period, one worker in five came to be employed in the making of capital goods. In financial terms, about 20 per cent of the national income was saved and invested, most of it in private enterprise, including railroads and utilities. A similar cycle prevailed in Europe.

The first world war interrupted this rhythm. It was never recaptured abroad. Here we seemed to have recaptured it in the 1920's, but on a somewhat different basis. It lasted seven years, followed by the worst depression in our history, and then chronic stagnation with a fifth of our working people unemployed.

Venture Capital

During the expanding century, investment was considered synonymous with risk, and investors took chances which

[1] Thomas C. Cochran and William Miller, *The Age of Enterprise,* Mac-millan, 1942.

would paralyze our modern cautious trust officers. A safe 3 per cent was not so popular as double your money or bust. Risk-taking was in the air, and winners had the odds on their side. You bought in a property on the 60 million population level, and sold out on the 80 million level. Ask any real estate dealer what the probabilities of profit are in this situation. Those who lost their shirts contributed just as effectively to closing the circuit as did the winners. If they put their money into wooden nutmegs or guessed wrong on a railroad terminal, the money was none the less *spent*. The dollars were not lost to the community as a whole; they kept on making the rounds.

Into canals, railroads, new cities, mines, rolling mills, lumber mills, wheat lands, oil fields, went the savings of America, and some from Europe as well, for we were a debtor nation. Capital was in huge demand. Whoever tightened his belt and added to the fund, helped to build up the country. Monetary thrift, accordingly, came to be classed with the eternal virtues, but what we might call monetary daring, the gambler's courage, was close behind it.

I did not happen to plunge in the stock market in the soaring twenties, but I was persuaded for various reasons to put some savings into the following ventures: (1) a patented kitchen mixer—which got mixed with the patents of a large corporation, jealous of its rights; (2) a platinum mine in northern Canada—which froze up; (3) a southern oil well —which practically reached the center of the earth before we would admit that we were licked. I still have some pretty certificates. But the oil drillers, the miners, the factory workers and the lawyers got my dollars, and they passed them on for bread, beans and potatoes. I take what satisfaction I may in the fact that I did my bit to keep the circuit closed. I did not hoard my savings; I put them to work. Every loser does the same if he invests in enterprises which make jobs.

My little flings with venture capital were not so typical of the 1920's as of the period before World War I. In 1910, all savings institutions had assets of only $16 billion. In 1937, they had $69 billions of savings, divided as follows:

Life insurance companies	$28,775,000,000
Time deposits in commercial banks	14,359,000,000
Mutual savings banks	11,572,000,000
Building and loan associations	5,712,000,000
Government funds, postal savings and baby bonds	8,659,000,000
Total	$69,077,000,000 [2]

After the war, as life grew more complicated, we gave our savings increasingly to these great institutions and trusted that they would invest the money for us. Sometimes they did, and sometimes they did not. They are a more cautious lot than the hero of the classical economists, the venture capital man. In the 1930's, the great institutions were loaded down with quantities of our cash which they could not, or dared not, invest.

World War I

In 1914 a depression was developing. It might have become serious, if orders from the Allies for food and munitions had not come flooding in from Europe. By 1916 we were back to substantially full employment. When we entered the war in April 1917, the dollars really began to roll. Some 25 per cent

2. Oscar L. Altman, *Saving, Investment, and National Income,* TNEC Monograph No. 37, 1941.

of our man power was drawn off into the Army, Navy and munitions industries, but the standards of living of the mass of the people actually rose. Everybody had a job, and everybody had money to spend. There was very little rationing.

How did the circuit work in wartime? Up to the end of 1921, the war had cost the United States some $36 billions.[3] Most of this outlay was met by a series of great bond issues, to a total of $22.8 billions. The balance, or a little more than a third of all, came from taxes, mostly income and excess profits taxes. Some of the bonds were placed with the commercial banks, who gave the government bank money in return and thus pumped new dollars into the system. Methods of controlling inflation were primitive, and wages followed prices in an ascending spiral. By 1920, many commodities had doubled in price over 1915, and the High Cost of Living was as familiar a phrase as Remember Pearl Harbor is now.

When the books were closed, it was found that many of the new dollars had come to rest in corporation surpluses, as the result of large war profits, and in the bank accounts of the well to do. Many manual workers lived better while the war lasted, but by the time the short, sharp depression of 1921-1922 had got through with them, their Liberty Bonds and other savings were pretty well cleaned out. We were left with a national debt of $25 billions. In 1914, the debt had been only one billion.

The dollar circuit had been closed magnificently by great injections of deficit financing. Indeed it had been more than closed, as the inflation bore eloquent witness. In Europe, inflation was far worse than it was here.

3. Figures prepared from annual reports of the Secretary of the Treasury, presented at TNEC hearings, May 1939, and reported in Monograph No. 37.

The Big Boom

Prosperity lasted seven years after the depression of 1921, from late 1922 to the stock market collapse in the fall of 1929. As the Brookings Institution pointed out, savings, especially in the higher income groups, were large throughout the period. Tremendous sums found their way into the great savings institutions, as we noted earlier.

Meanwhile corporations more and more financed new plant and equipment from their own savings—internal accumulations from depreciation reserves and profits not distributed to stockholders. At the TNEC hearings in May 1939, Mr. Edward Stettinius, then of the Steel Corporation, testified that from 1921 through 1938 his company had invested no less than $1,220,000,000 in plant and equipment, and that 96 per cent of it came from internal funds of the corporation, not from outside sources.

Mr. Leon Henderson asked: "You are not at any time in the immediate future going to give any great amount of business to underwriting firms; you are not going to tap individual savings very much?"

Mr. Stettinius replied: "That is correct."

Dr. Oscar Altman during the same hearings presented charts which summarized the situation for *all* American corporations. From 1923 through 1929, they invested an average of $8.5 billions each year in plant and equipment. Of this amount, $6.4 billions, or 75 per cent, came from internal sources. According to the studies of Dr. Fabricant of the National Bureau of Economic Research, depreciation and depletion allowances alone, for all American corporations, amounted to $5 billions in 1929. In that year only $2 billions of new productive capital was obtained from outside sources.

It is clear from these figures that corporations were doing much of their own saving, thank you, and did not need your savings and mine, at least on the old scale. Good accounting practice in recent years demands that depreciation allowances be set aside annually, whatever the earnings of the company. Evidently we have encountered here a basic reason for the decline in opportunities to invest the savings of the general public. It makes no difference to the workings of our economy as a whole, of course, whether savings are made by individuals out of their own incomes or by corporations out of profits which they might have paid out in dividends or higher salaries. The point is whether *total* savings exceed *total* investments.

The Rate of Savings

Gross savings for the period, including the internal savings of corporations, have been estimated by Dr. Lauchlin Currie as follows:[4]

	Gross National Income (In Billions)	Estimated Savings	Per Cent of National Income
1922	$64.3	$11.2	17.4
1923	74.8	15.1	20.2
1924	75.2	14.7	19.6
1925	79.7	15.5	19.4
1926	84.8	16.7	19.7
1927	82.7	15.6	18.9
1928	86.2	15.5	18.0
1929	90.0	16.9	18.8

Thus during the age of jazz, flaming youth and flagpole

4. TNEC Monograph No. 37, 1941. Gross national income, as we noted on page 10, is larger than the figure usually quoted as "national income"; the difference represents depreciation and depletion allowances, etc.

sitters—the age, you remember, when stern moralists were telling us that we were wallowing in soft luxuries—the American people were salting down from 17 to 20 per cent of all the income they received. Roughly half the total was saved by corporations, half by individuals.

This situation put the dollar circuit, so to speak, on the spot. Where were productive investments to match this colossal thrift? Could private plant and equipment absorb it all? It could not. Despite the growth of the automobile, radio and electrical industries, despite new skyscrapers towering high above many towns which had no real need of them, the investment in private plant and equipment absorbed only 53 per cent of our total savings during these eight years, according to Dr. Currie.

Where Did the Savings Go?

This left a wide gulf to be filled. Where did the balance of our savings go? Into five major channels: (1) residential housing; (2) government highways, schools, public works; (3) foreign loans; (4) financing installment buying; (5) building up inventories.

The war had left us with a housing shortage which absorbed billions until it was made up—made up, at least, to the point where profits in housing developments were no longer attractive. In 1927, the housing boom began to taper off. In Florida it collapsed with a resounding bang.

The federal government, under Secretary Mellon, was retiring some of its war debt during the period, but this deflationary measure was offset by deficit financing on the part of states and cities, primarily to build roads for the new automobiles to run on.

Foreign loans by citizens and corporations soared in the 1920's. Not until 1928 did the hopeful investors begin to feel a cold draft about their necks. By 1930 they were frozen stiff. Observe, however, that they had made their honest contribution to close the dollar circuit. Their savings were advanced, let us say, to Poland, but the dollars probably never left this country. They were deposited in a New York bank. Poland ordered machinery, motor cars, victrolas, or whatever it might be, and the dollars were paid to American businessmen and workers. Even if Poland took the dollars and spent them in France, in due course Frenchmen would buy American goods, with the same beneficent effects on the circuit. Only when the investors wanted their interest or principal did the foreign loans become bad news. This illustrates again the little understood fact that losses suffered by individual investors are not necessarily losses for the economy as a whole.

Installment credit represents a use of the nation's savings only when the total of loans is going up. From 1923 to 1929 the total was going up, from 1930 to 1933 it was coming down. This type of investment is only a temporary shot in the arm, with no future to it. The limit of installment credit has hovered around $6 to $8 billions. We reached this ceiling in 1929.

Inventory accumulations are even less reliable than installment credit as permanent offsets to savings. These goods in warehouses or on merchants' shelves go up and they go down, often very rapidly. They are not like a solid dam or a factory which is there ready for work all the time. The best kind of investments, from the point of view of the dollar circuit, are those which not only put men to work while they are being built, but keep men at useful tasks after they are built.

Savings and the Stock Market

What about the stock market; did it not absorb savings at a great rate? It did, but the only people it put to work were customers' men, astrologers and investment counselors, who instructed us in how to lose our money scientifically. The security markets in their role as gambling houses—they have other more useful roles as well—are a kind of circuit within a circuit, where the transfer rate of numbers is prodigious, but nothing productive happens, except perhaps the stimulation of the luxury trades. Confidence, however, may be generated by the activity of these markets, with good effects on more tangible investments.

Six men, sitting down to an all-night poker game, give us a small model of this phenomenon. Money changes hands rapidly; some gain, some lose; but the dollars stay within a closed circuit. The only productive spending involved is when the kitty finances another case of beer.

It is important to get clear that the only investments which buy the wheelbarrows are those which put saved dollars into the hands of people who will go to the warehouse and spend for potatoes. This means normally into the hands of people who work. Savings which go into any kind of gambling, whether in stocks or lands or poker chips or commodities, tend to become tangled in a paper spiral. The net effect may be equivalent to hoarding, by holding money out of productive use.

It was not the panic on the stock market in October 1929 which broke the dollar circuit and plunged us into the depression. The circuit was in precarious balance before that, because of the end of the housing boom, the decline of foreign loans, the ceilings reached in installment credit and in inventory accumulations. Opportunities for investment at the scale required to balance savings had dried up. There would have been a depression without the stock market crash, though not such a spectacular one.

The depression was indeed world-wide. Natives in remote jungles gathering copra felt its blasts, as well as the unhappy citizens of Wall Street. Presently bankers began to call their loans, pulling dollars out of the system, and making matters worse. People stopped spending as though their right hands were paralyzed. The rules of the circuit were violated at a hundred points. So it virtually ceased to function.

8

THE CIRCUIT SLOWS DOWN

In the 1930's, the dollar circuit went through two phases—violent contraction, followed by moderate expansion. In the latter phase there were more dollars in the system than in the 1920's, but they never moved as fast. In the first phase, the rate of transfer was glacierlike; in the second, like a sluggish stream, and so it remained until the war orders of the 1940's. The phases are dramatically shown in a continuation of Dr. Currie's figures:

Savings in the Depression

	Gross National Income[1] (In Billions)	Estimated Savings	Per Cent Savings to National Income
Down phase			
1929	$90.0	$16.9	18.8
1930	79.8	13.8	17.3
1931	63.9	9.5	14.8
1932	47.4	4.8	10.1
1933	46.2	2.8	6.0

1. Net national income was $82 billions in 1929, and close to $40 billions in 1933, the low point.

	Gross National Income	Estimated Savings	Per Cent Savings to National Income
	(In Billions)		
Up phase			
1934	55.8	4.3	7.8
1935	61.7	8.4	13.7
1936	69.8	13.1	18.8
1937	78.2	15.0	19.2
1938	70.9	10.8	15.2

Gross national income was cut from $90 billions in 1929 to $46 billions in 1933—almost exactly in half. It recovered to $78 billions in 1937, then dropped to $71 billions in 1938, primarily because of the checking of public works and other government outlays. For a time in 1937, the federal budget was actually balanced; receipts exceeded disbursements.

The Down Phase

Savings, the table shows, fell with the national income, and climbed with it. In the blackest year, 1933, we still saved 6 per cent of the national income. By 1937 we had climbed to 19.2 per cent—the ratio of the prosperous 1920's. As national income falls, most people are forced to spend relatively more of their personal income for food and shelter, often drawing on past savings to keep going. Loans are made on life insurance policies, savings bank accounts are cleaned out, stocks and bonds are thrown on the market for what they will fetch. The more fortunate citizens tend to hoard any surplus of income they receive, while the nervous ones draw out currency and even gold from the banks and put it in safe deposit boxes. The net effect is a lower ratio of saving to national income, but more straight hoarding of what is saved.

In the down phase, all the investment opportunities that

had helped absorb our savings in the twenties showed a drastic decline. Businessmen reduced their outlays for plant and equipment. Foreign lending practically ceased. Hardly any new houses were built. Installment buying went into reverse. State and local governments made heavy cuts in their budgets for highways and other public works. The federal government expanded its outlays slightly, but not nearly enough to offset these reductions.

So less and less money was spent, fewer and fewer goods were bought. The whole financial system ground to a standstill when the banks closed in March 1933. Bank money had ceased to operate.

The Up Phase

Mr. Roosevelt got the banks functioning again by applying some unusual pressures. He took us off the gold standard, gradually depreciated the dollar in terms of gold, and insured bank deposits. A certain measure of confidence returned. In 1934 the upward phase began. It was inaugurated and sustained by the spending of the federal government—for public works, relief, RFC loans, loans to homeowners, AAA payments to farmers, and the rest.

From 1931 through 1938, the federal debt increased by $21 billions, reflecting these outlays. Many harsh words were spoken about government spending, of which "boondoggling" was one of the mildest. Some of the projects were foolish enough, but that was not the main point. The main point was the attempt to close the dollar circuit. Spending for any project, even bailing out Great Salt Lake, would have furthered this end. A study of a billion dollars disbursed by the PWA revealed that after contractors had taken their profit and paid the balance out to workers, the workers spent it as follows:

For food	$350 million
For shelter	244 "
For clothing	130 "
For transportation (mostly automobile)	109 "
For recreation	65 "
For health services	50 "

The claim checks got back to the warehouse, and close to a billion dollars' worth of savings were offset.

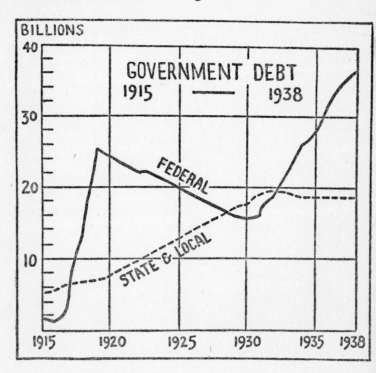

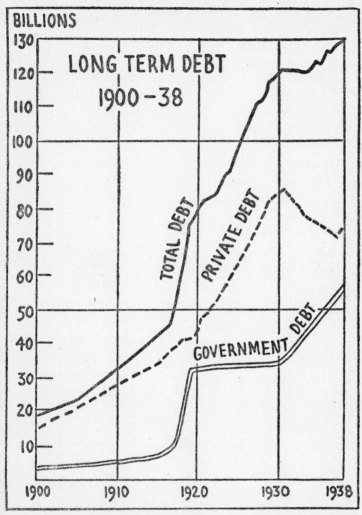

BILLIONS

LONG TERM DEBT 1900-38

TOTAL DEBT

PRIVATE DEBT

GOVERNMENT DEBT

130 120 110 100 90 80 70 60 50 40 30 20 10

1900 1910 1920 1930 1938

Charts based on figures from the Department of Commerce and the Treasury.
Reproduced from the author's *Idle Money, Idle Men*, Harcourt, Brace, 1941.

During the 1920's, federal debt had declined while local debt increased, leaving total government debt about on a level. Private long-term debt, however, had gone up like the side of Vesuvius. In the 1930's, the curves were reversed. Federal debt took on the outlines of Vesuvius, local government debt leveled off, and private debt performed an accomplished swan dive.

The Failure of Pump Priming

What happened is clear enough. In the 1920's our savings were invested primarily in private long-term debt, including foreign loans and housing mortgages. In the 1930's, as private debt declined, the federal government deliberately attempted to offset savings and close the gap. The effort was not altogether successful. The government never spent enough to overcome stagnation and unemployment. Pump priming failed as such. Private investment picked up after 1934, but not sufficiently to take over the burden from the government. Stronger medicine than pump priming was needed. The role of the government can be shown in the following figures, taken from Dr. Currie's testimony:

	Percentage	
Expenditures as Offsets to Savings	Six Prosperous Years 1923-28	Three Recovery Years 1935-37
Private plant	53	44
Government outlays	3	20
Housing	32	9
Inventory accumulation	5	19
Installment buying increases	4	8
Foreign loans	3	0
Total	100	100

Mr. Henry S. Dennison presented charts at the TNEC hearings to show the relation between public and private outlays for construction work alone, including maintenance. During the 1920's public construction ran from 20 to 25 per cent of all. In 1933 it rose to 50 per cent of all. In 1938 it stood at 44 per cent. Despite this relative increase, the dollar total for public construction was no greater in 1938 than in 1930.

Contrary to popular belief, the government (federal and local combined) did not spend appreciably more for construction in the middle 1930's than in the late 1920's. But it *maintained its expenditures,* while private construction, especially housing, declined drastically. The result, of course, was a far higher government ratio, and a net decline for the economy as a whole. On this formula, stagnation and unemployment were bound to continue. The idle money bred idle men.

At the time the banks closed, there were a thousand or more self-help groups in the country, using claim checks of their own devising. They worked, after a fashion, but the trouble was that they could not be exchanged for legal dollars. No self-help group can provide for all its food and supplies in our highly specialized economy. I visited some of these little potato communities and wrote an article about them. It was pathetic to see them trying so hard to do what could not be done. They were a hundred years too late. America, for better or for worse, is now a single economic organism, and must swim or sink as a unit.

Monopoly as a Barrier

Another difficulty in the attempt to get back to normal employment was due to monopoly, and the so-called "administered prices" of large corporate groups. These groups were outside the free market; they more or less set their own prices. As the depression deepened, they dismissed their workers in great numbers, but they did not reduce their prices much. Two companies, for instance, control sulphur production in the United States. From 1926 to 1938, the price of sulphur never quivered from $18 a ton.[2] The price of wheat tumbled to 30 cents a bushel, but the price of farm machinery held its own. Wheat was subject to extreme competition, while the prices of farm machinery were "administered."

These policies dealt buying power a double blow: the discharged workers lost their wages, while those still employed were discouraged by the relatively high prices still prevailing.

Labor unions, trade associations and other pressure groups also tried to shield their wages or prices from the cold blasts of free competition, and many succeeded. If the market had not been full of "sticky prices," the depression would not have been so severe.

Explanations Which Failed to Explain

Not many citizens saw clearly what was going on in the early years of the depression. We were all stunned by the mountain that had fallen on us, and we did some things which in retrospect look strange indeed.

To begin with, we pretended that nothing had happened. On January 24, 1930, three months after the big gong sounded on Wall Street, a New York newspaper came out with these headlines:

Trade Recovery Now Complete, President Told.

2. For a full account of this monopoly, see Robert H. Montgomery, *The Brimstone Game*, Vanguard, 1940.

Business Survey Conference Reports Industry Has Progressed By Own Power.

No Stimulants Needed.

Progress In All Lines by the Early Spring Is Forecast.

On December 10, 1929, Charles M. Schwab said: "Never before has American business been as firmly entrenched for prosperity as it is today." On October 16, 1930, he said: "Looking to the future I see in the further acceleration of science continuous jobs for our workers." Not until February 7, 1931, did he give up and admit: "I am not predicting anything."

On August 17, 1930, Henry Ford was still undaunted: "I, personally, am very hopeful because I think the country has ceased to be sick, is now well, and will soon be strong and active again." These statements, of course, were deliberately intended to restore confidence and reverse the trend, but they did not work.

When it became evident that thinking the right thoughts was not putting smoke in factory chimneys, all kinds of campaigns were launched for "economy." Economy!—which was precisely the disease that the dollar circuit was expiring of. We were told by earnest gentlemen that prosperity had been a drunkard's spree and that now we must sober up and get along with bare essentials. It would do us, and the economic system, good. They did not stop to think what would happen to the makers of automobiles, refrigerators, radios, moving pictures, electric power, gasoline, if we all stopped buying these products.

A determined drive was also made to lower wages, on the theory that if costs were thereby reduced, businessmen would be encouraged to produce more. It was part of the philosophy to let the depression heal itself by shaking out certain "sticky" elements, get to the bottom, and then start up automatically. This philosophy had worked in earlier depressions. In 1932, however, with the national income cut in half, no man could say where the bottom would be. J. M. Keynes saw the logical end of such drives:

If we carry "economy" of every kind to its logical conclusion, we shall find that we have balanced the budget at naught on both sides, with all of us flat on our backs starving to death from a refusal, for reasons of economy, to buy one another's services.[3]

There was human flesh and blood to be considered. People could endure only so much. The demand to make them endure more, because somewhere in the depths there might be an automatic turning point, was too uncertain and too cruel. No one could prove that there was such a point. But it could be proved—and was—that government spending could relieve the depression whenever the word was given. Despite this proof, "spending" throughout the depression continued to be a disreputable word.

Mr. Roosevelt in his 1932 campaign hoped that he could balance the budget, amid the applause of the highest authorities. It was a pious hope, but nothing could have been more fatal to the dollar circuit. If federal offsets to savings were cut off, the only element which might restore the circuit would be gone. Depression would indeed become bottomless. The theory was that the act of balancing the budget would so stimulate confidence that businessmen would promptly take our savings and enlarge their plants.

Businessmen Are Not Fools

The studies of the Brookings Institution cited earlier show

3. John Maynard Keynes, *Essays in Persuasion,* Harcourt, Brace, 1932.

that it just could not happen. Plants are enlarged when business is good. Competent businessmen do not expand their factories because of moral acts in Washington. They expand when their sales are increasing, and their sales in 1932 were going to the damnation bow-wows. Look again at Mr. Currie's figures for national income. Mr. Roosevelt changed his views about the budget, but many others did not—until the war shelved the whole discussion and restored "spending" to respectability.

Another drive was launched for cheaper capital. It was hoped that by reducing interest rates and making credit "easy," businessmen would come into the market for loans. But again, competent businessmen have no use for loans, even at zero per cent, when their stock of goods is freezing up. Interest rates fell throughout the period—as they have been falling for a generation—but the effect in encouraging new capital outlays was negligible. The economy had gone far beyond the point where such weak medicine could effect a cure.

A similar discussion raged around the matter of plant obsolescence. It was pointed out that thirty, fifty, eighty billions could well be invested in bringing plant and equipment up to date, thus increasing its productivity. Perhaps it could in Utopia, but not in a world where the present plant was operating at something like half of its capacity. Increasing plant capacity in the depths of a depression is always fine for the other fellow, but not for any particular businessman still certified as sane.

Afraid of the Impossible

Perhaps the most curious of all the agitations, seen in

retrospect, was the widespread terror of inflation. This fear seized the country as the federal debt began to rise. I remember debating the subject, along about 1935, with a distinguished financier who worked himself and the audience into such a panic that I began to have misgivings myself. I was defeated hands down. Yet there was not the remotest chance of a runaway inflation when millions of our citizens were unemployed. As Dr. Hansen puts it:

The fact is that no price inflation is possible so long as vast unemployed resources of men and machines can be drawn upon to produce an ever-increasing output of goods and services. So long as there are unused resources, every increase in demand is matched by an increase in supply. Thus any incipient price rise is held in check. There can be no general price inflation until scarcity conditions, owing to full employment, become general over a considerable range of industry.[4]

In Summary

It is fascinating to follow the historical course of the dollar circuit. Its behavior is almost completely mechanical. If the claim checks do not get back, the potatoes are not cleared. How they get back is immaterial. Any method will do, even printing currency. But some methods, like running the printing presses, are far worse than others for the cycles which follow.

The circuit was closed before 1914, mostly by investment in private enterprises on a continuously expanding scale, along with the expansion of land and population. Dangerous slowdowns occurred, as when the era of transcontinental railroad building came to an end, but they were always repaired without chronic stagnation.

4. Alvin H. Hansen, *Full Recovery or Stagnation,* Norton, 1938.

War outlays closed the circuit from 1915 to 1920. In fact too many dollars were injected, the result was serious inflation. We recovered from the effects here, but in Germany and Russia, inflation ran clean off the map, while in France and Italy the currency had to be devalued, wiping out the investments of the middle class.

Our seven years' prosperity after the war was not shared abroad—except for the brief and spotty assistance of our loans. These same loans helped the circuit here, together with the housing boom, installment buying, inventory accumulations, and the expansion of the automobile industry, with its collateral highway construction. Prosperity collapsed when these outlets for savings were saturated. Government interference had nothing to do with the collapse; the confidence of investors in Hoover was no less than their confidence in Harding and Coolidge. In his farewell address to Congress on December 4, 1928, President Coolidge said:

The great wealth created by our enterprise and industry, and saved by our economy, has had the widest distribution among our own people, and has gone out in a steady stream to serve the charity and the business of the world. The requirements of existence have passed beyond the standard of necessity into the region of luxury. Enlarging production is consumed by an increasing demand at home, and an expanding commerce abroad. The country can regard the present with satisfaction, and anticipate the future with optimism.

This was less than a year before the Wall Street explosion, but it reflected the almost unanimous attitude of business and financial leaders.

The depression apparently had no bottom on a policy of waiting for automatic recovery. That policy was tested for more than three years. Only when the federal government began to offset savings by a positive program of credit control and spending was the spiral reversed. Without this action, the rules of the dollar circuit indicate that we should have been driven to rationing, or to chaos. Not until the war came, however, did the government spend enough to generate all-out production and full employment.

9
DOLLARS IN WAR

THE TASK OF FINANCE in war," says the London *Economist,* "is to see that nothing is decided on financial grounds." The fifth Lend-Lease Report concurs: "The normal considerations of international commerce, finance and foreign exchange, are not permitted to interfere with fundamental war needs."

These statements emphasize that there are no immutable "laws" in the financial world, national or international. A law is something you cannot monkey with, whatever happens. We cannot set aside the laws of ballistics to give our guns longer range in wartime. But we can set aside the "law" of supply and demand—and every warring nation has done so. It is not possible, however, to set aside for very long the limitations of the dollar circuit, if money is to be used at all. These limits are perhaps as close to financial "laws" as we can get.

Control Levers in Reverse

Marriner Eccles, Chairman of the Federal Reserve Board, has given us a dramatic account of how war reverses the control levers of the circuit.[1] Some people thought that Mr. Eccles was an inveterate "spender," because he advocated

1. *Fortune,* August 1941.

more government outlays during the depression. They are surprised and a little shocked to find that he has now turned into an implacable "saver." Small minds may accuse him of inconsistency, but there is no more consistent follower of the principles of the dollar circuit than Mr. Eccles. If he calls for different action now, it is because he realizes that when the tub is full of water it is time to turn off the faucet.

For ten years, he says, we have been struggling to overcome deflation. Now we must struggle against inflation.

We have tried to discourage savings. Now we must encourage them.

We have used deficit financing to good effect. Now there is no sense in it, and it should be kept to the minimum consistent with the war effort.

We have tried to stimulate public works. Now we should cut them to the bone.

There is no inconsistency here. When the economy is on part time, with great unemployment, the task of financial administrators is to increase the rate of spending and investment. When the economy is on full time, with little or no unemployment, their task is to hold down the rate of spending, lest inflation upset the system.

Armistice Among Economists

Indeed, now that capacity operation has come, there is no longer a real quarrel between "spenders" like Mr. Eccles, Alvin Hansen, John Maynard Keynes, and the more orthodox economists. Both camps are united on a number of points. They agree that we must impose high taxes, stimulate or "force" savings, avoid borrowing from the banks any more than is absolutely necessary, control wages and prices, and ration scarce goods.

The camps divided originally because the orthodox economists assumed that a part-time economy could not long continue; automatic action would soon right it. The Keynes school believed that a part-time economy might become chronic unless positive action were taken in the direction of offsetting idle savings. Now that the two schools have got together, on the field of battle as it were, one sincerely hopes that they can stay together. We are going to need every competent economist we can lay hold of before this war and its aftermath have run their course.

How Germany Pays For the War

Germany has been operating a war economy for almost a decade. Let us follow Dal Hitchcock and watch the wheels go round.[2]

When Hitler came to power, a third of all German workers were unemployed, debts were unmanageable, and a mood of despair prevailed. The dreadful inflation of 1923 was a haunting memory. Hitler called Dr. Hjalmar Schacht as financial adviser. In 1934 he launched a huge government spending program for public works and rearmament. Financial authorities in other countries said that Germany would be bankrupt in a few months as a result of this action. Where was the money to come from? That was nine years ago, and Germany is still solvent. The great housing and highway projects have been built, together with the most terrible war machine the world has ever seen.

Some people discount this achievement by saying that it

2. *Harper's*, February 1941. This account is the clearest that I have seen. Data are hard to get, and it will remain for history to disclose the full story of German financing. Since the war began, the Nazis have made full use of the assets of conquered nations.

is a fiat structure, enforced by the boots of the Gestapo. Mr. Hitchcock believes that such discounting amounts to dangerous wishful thinking. "The Nazis were forced to do the impossible financially, and the fact that they have succeeded makes it essential that we understand what they have done." Dr. Schacht borrowed ideas from both Keynes and the great Swedish economist, Gustav Cassel. He moved cautiously at first, putting the new theories into tangible operation.

He began by issuing short-term government notes. These were deposited with the Reichsbank (akin to our Federal Reserve), which opened checking accounts for the government, thus creating new bank money. The government used the money to order tanks, let us say, from Krupp, at a good price. Krupp put unemployed men to work, paid out wages, and had a nice profit left. The company was then "invited"— a touch of the strong arm here—to use its nice profit for the purchase of long-term government bonds. When the invitation was accepted, Krupp's check went to the Reichsbank and the original notes were canceled. Krupp was given bonds, but bank money was squeezed out of the circuit, and the danger of inflation was reduced. The government debt of course stayed up. Along with the government spending went government regimentation. Wages and salaries were frozen at depression levels—and really frozen, along with prices.

Next Dr. Schacht clamped down on currency expansion by getting excess currency converted into government bonds and stamps. The conversion was presently hastened by a forced savings program, similar to the program that the British have —and to the one that we shall probably have.[3] Subscriptions for bonds were deducted from pay rolls.

3. See John Maynard Keynes, *How to Pay for the War*, Harcourt, 1940.

Profits were encouraged, but Schacht saw to it that all savings were promptly invested either in government bonds or in new plant and equipment. The money circuit was kept turning at a strong, even rate. No idle money was permitted to accumulate. While Keynes was expounding ideas on this subject, the Germans were putting them into practice. Without rigid enforcement of wage, price and cost controls, however, inflation would have wrecked the whole program. "The belief has been widespread that there was something mysterious, or even miraculous about the German armament achievement. . . . It was nothing of the sort. . . . The achievement was rendered possible by holding civilian consumption . . . close to . . . minimum levels . . . and diverting to armament production nearly all of the increment to national income which resulted from the full employment of men, materials, and equipment."[4]

The Principles of War Finance

Similar financial stories could be told for Britain,[5] Canada, Australia, Italy, Japan. The principles of war finance are simple, however complicated the technical details.

First, money must be made immediately available for the equipment of the armed services, up to the limit of industrial capacity.

4. Crum, *et al., Fiscal Planning for Total War,* National Bureau, 1942.
5. A London dispatch by David Anderson in *The New York Times,* April 26, 1942, describes the control of inflation in Britain. "Here is how it works: The British people today are carrying in their pockets more cash than ever before, and at the same time have less to spend it on. This would be an ideal set-up for inflation were the public able to compete in the face of rising prices. But they are not. The government applies a three-way brake in the form of (1) taxation, (2) savings campaigns, (3) the strictest rationing of consumers' goods. Thus the government syphons off most of the surplus cash, and has managed to keep price levels even."

Second, provision must be made for a minimum standard of life for the rest of the population. Otherwise morale will suffer. Cold and hungry citizens cannot produce their quota of munitions.

Third, war costs should be met so far as possible by taxation. As the stock of consumer goods declines, while wage and salary levels remain high, taxes are easier to pay during the war than after it. They are also positive guards against inflation.

Fourth, the next best thing to taxes is the sale of bonds to the public, which are paid for *with dollars already in the circuit.* This method is also anti-inflationary. It does, however, increase the government debt, while taxes do not. If the public will not buy enough bonds voluntarily, then forced savings are in order.

Fifth, in so far as taxes and bond sales to the public fail to cover war costs, the balance must be raised by borrowing from the commercial banks, or from the central bank—the Federal Reserve. For every dollar so borrowed, as we saw earlier, a new dollar of bank money is shot into the system. This is the raw fuel of inflation, and the method should be held to a minimum. It was not held down in the last war, and the world has been suffering from the results ever since.

Sixth, inflation can also be checked by *direct* methods—price fixing, wage and salary fixing, rent fixing, priorities, and by rationing consumers' goods. The aim is to find methods which produce the fewest complaints, the smallest opportunity for evasion, and some approach to equality of sacrifice. Such methods were only crudely used in the last war. Both Germany and Britain are streamlining them in this war.

Seventh, large loans to foreign governments should be

avoided. The friendlier the governments, the more resolutely should we deny them credit. Our allies can never repay large loans, and no better method has ever been devised to turn friends into enemies. Make gifts or swaps—not formal loans. Lend-lease follows this rule.

Paying For the War in America

How well is the United States following these principles? Not so well as Britain and Canada but better than China— where inflation has got badly out of hand, with some prices up forty-fold since 1937.[6]

Suppose we cast a rough model of the dollar circuit for 1943, as forecast by high authorities at the beginning of that year. A glance at it will tell us where the trouble is. Remember that there is no trouble about getting all the money we need to pay for guns and tanks. The trouble lies in the future, especially in the threat of further inflation.

Just five figures will give the over-all picture for 1943.[7]

		(In Billions)	
(1)	Expenses for war, estimated at	$80	
(2)	Civilian goods and services	60	
	Total gross national income		$140
(3)	Federal taxes at 1942 rates	$20	
(4)	Sales of bonds to the public (old money) at 1942 rates	12	
(5)	New dollars to be borrowed from the banks	48	
	Total to meet war bill		$80
	Increase in government debt (4+5)	$60	

6. Wendell L. Willkie, *One World,* Simon and Schuster, 1943.

7. As this book goes to press it looks as if the ratio of taxes to war outlays might be pushed up to 33 per cent, and that sales of bonds to the public might also show a higher ratio. This will not affect the general principles we are trying to establish.

What is wrong with this picture? Plenty. Not nearly
enough of the war cost is being met by taxes, not nearly
enough by bond sales to the public, far too much by borrowing from the banks. There appear to be 48 billion dollars of
potential inflation in the picture as it stands—though we shall
find some qualifications later. By contrast, look at the approx-
imate picture for Britain today, in percentages:

	Percentage
Met by taxes[8]	50
Met by bond sales to public (including forced savings)	25
Met by borrowings from the banks	25
Total war cost	100

Can We Do as Well as Britain?

To do as well as Britain, we should have to double our
taxes and turn over $40 billions to the government instead of
$20 billions. We should have to increase public subscriptions
to bonds—with probably a forced savings plan to help us—
to $20 billions instead of the present $12 billions. In this
way bank borrowings could be reduced from $48 billions to
$20 billions. The five figures would then look like this:

		(In Billions)	
(1)	War expenses as before	$80	
(2)	Civilian goods and services as before	60	
	Total gross national income		$140
(3)	Taxes at revised rates	$40	
(4)	Sales of bonds to public at revised rates	20	
(5)	New dollars borrowed from banks	20	
	Total to meet war bill		$80
	Increase in government debt	$40	

8. In New Zealand 67 per cent of war costs are met by taxes.

In this picture the government debt increases by $40 billions instead of $60 billions, while the pressure for inflation is greatly reduced. How great is the pressure? It is impossible to set an exact figure, but we can venture a guess, based on the original five figures for 1943.

The Inflationary Gap

If $80 billions of war expense and $60 billions of civilian goods and services are paid for at current prices, it follows that $140 billions will be received during the year by the workers, farmers, the manufacturers and stockholders—in short, the people of the United States. The people make the goods and receive the wages, salaries, interest, profits, which form the money outgo for the costs. They have in their pockets the full amount to "buy the goods back" on the good old potato principle. This, we remember, was one statement, at least, on which all economists could agree. The act of production automatically creates the income to clear it.

The people take out of their pockets $20 billions for federal taxes, $12 billions for buying bonds. That leaves $108 billions in the national pocket. Out of this some old debts will be paid off, which is bound to result in liquidating a certain amount of bank loans, and will thus reduce bank money in the system. Bank statements show that this is actually taking place. It will act as an offset to the 48 billions of new dollars created by government borrowing. Also out of the national pocket some money will be invested in civilian enterprises, some will be set aside as reserves by corporations, and some will be hoarded.[9]

9. *The New York Times,* November 15, 1942, carried a story on the high rate of hoarding in 1942.

Assume for example that these payments out of the national pocket for retiring loans, for investing, for reserves and for hoarding, amounted to $18 billions—a guess, but I think a conservative one. Then $90 billions would be left in the national pocket with which to buy civilian goods. But if the civilian goods produced amounted to only $60 billions, as assumed in the table, then there would be an "inflationary gap," or excess pressure, of $30 billions.

Some $90 billions of hot money may be trying to buy $60 billions of goods. Price ceilings are likely to be shattered right and left. If they somehow hold, then black markets appear in back streets, like speakeasies during Prohibition. *Time* describes black markets in gasoline, sugar and tires.[10] "In New York City, OPA broke up a gas-coupon pool that sounded like the Al Capone days, including gangsters called 'Red,' 'Lefty,' 'The Mutt,' and 'Bananas.' A Utica ring stole 8,450 B and C books, peddled them through a long chain of racketeers, who kept hijacking each other." Black markets in meat are a national problem as I write. The country will be crawling with this kind of thing if we have a lot more money in our pockets than we can spend for the goods available at prices fixed by the OPA.

But if we can achieve the British ratio for paying war costs, the inflation boiler rapidly loses its pressure. Pickings for "Lefty" and "Bananas" become scarce. If we could drain off from the national pocket $20 billions more in taxes, and $8 billions more in bonds, then the $30 billions of steam calculated above would drop to $2 billions—a negligible figure. The Reichsbank claims it has reduced inflationary pressure to zero. That is the challenge we have to meet.

10. December 21, 1942.

Paying for the War in Utopia

In Utopia, when they have a war, they pay for it completely out of current taxes, which eliminates both inflation and an increase in national debt. If the annual cost is 80, then Utopians hand over 80 out of the 140 they receive during the year. This leaves them 60 for food, clothing and shelter. But it leaves them nothing to retire debts, nothing to invest or save for any purpose. The political and administrative difficulties of collecting the full cost of the war out of taxes could be surmounted only in Utopia. In 1940, federal taxes totaled about $6 billions. Could we raise them to $80 billions in 1943? We could not. But we have raised them to $20 billions, and we could raise them to $40 billions. At least Britain, Canada and Germany have achieved that ratio.

The Spendings Tax

There is no painless way to increase taxes, any more than there is a painless way to win a military battle. But some ways are better than others, fairer to more people. Treasury officials have proposed a "spendings tax," which they claim is fairer to more people, and I am inclined to think that they are right. The details of administration may be complicated, but the principle is clear.

Each citizen figures out what he spends in a year for consumers' goods. Below a base line of subsistence—say $1,200 for a family—he pays no tax at all. Above that line he pays taxes that amount to, say, 10 per cent of his consumer goods spendings. Above a higher line, he pays, say, 20 per cent, and so on up. The more ritzy he becomes, the higher the percentage he pays. The effect would be to induce all of us to keep our spendings down to bedrock, and thus reduce the pressure for inflation. Yet everyone would be assured the essentials of life, completely untaxed. This is a great advantage over a general sales tax, which tends to "soak the poor."

You do not have to stand on your head or wrap one foot around the chandelier to understand the spendings tax, as some Congressmen have alleged. You compute your own spendings: your spendable assets at the beginning of the year plus your year's income and other cash receipts less savings and investments as defined by the Treasury, equals your spending for consumers' goods subject to taxation. The technical details of administering the tax are the Treasury's headache. They propose to combine it with the income tax.

The major alternatives are either a general sales tax—which hits the lower brackets hard—or stiffer rates and a broader base on the present income tax. I think the spendings tax is fairer than the current income tax, because it does not soak citizens on that part of their income which they invest in government bonds, in life insurance premiums, in paying off debts, or in productive enterprises. It soaks them only if they want to indulge in fancy standards of living.

Eighty Billions For Peace?

It is now proved that a modern nation can devote 60 per cent or more of its energy to the wastes of war, still live frugally on the remaining 40 per cent, and have no trouble about finding the money. There will be trouble later on, however, if the money is found by faulty methods. Nearly everyone who can work has a job, and most of us feel that we have a real place in the national economy, where before the war many of us felt that we had none.

Suppose we let our imaginations roam for a minute, and

consider a point in history where there is no more war. The dreadful thing is done with. The 60 per cent of the national effort which went for fighting and for bombers and TNT, can now be turned to prefabricated houses, health centers, private airplanes which land on a dime, cars with transparent plastic tops, super highways, research laboratories.[11]

A rise of some 50 per cent in living standards is indicated at this imaginary point in history. Everyone has a job, as in the war—though he works shorter hours. Everyone pays high taxes, as in the war. The federal government passes back part of the taxes for social security benefits, part for public works valuable in their own right. But let us suppose that the largest fraction of our taxes is distributed by the government to every family, rich and poor, in the form of rationing stamps for food, clothing, health, shelter—enough stamps to guarantee the essentials to every last person in the country. The stamps are good at any store, good for rent or its equivalent, good for medical care of any kind. Citizens can choose what they like within these four categories. Businessmen receiving the stamps turn them back via their bank to the Treasury for cash. The Treasury finds the cash from the taxes we have paid. There is no borrowing at all.

Let us leave the speculation here, without any more details, for it is another kind of point I want to make: We pay high taxes, but instead of underwriting a war with them, we underwrite our own security. Instead of howitzers we buy houses with them. At the same time we provide businessmen with a market nearly as vast as the war gives them, and far more dependable.

11. Substantially the budget proposed by Henry J. Kaiser in his historic speech before the National Association of Manufacturers, in December 1942.

Paying for the Peace in Utopia

I am not now advocating such a plan. Probably I never shall. It is simply a model to stretch our imaginations. It gives us a glimpse of what the dollar circuit could do if we really wanted to use it all out. The circuit operates to meet a similar situation today, except that the market is largely for economic waste. The imagined market would be for economic wealth, and it could be met equally well, especially as it would not be complicated with inflation or any increase in the public debt. It would be a pay-as-you-go market, in which the circuit would always be in balance. Dollars earned in the act of production would roll into the national pocket, that is, the people's pockets. They would roll out of the national pocket to the stores, and to the government as taxation. They roll back from the government to the people, somewhat redistributed in the form of stamps for the purchase of the essentials of life for everybody.

The chief difficulty with any such plan is that it requires new concepts about taxation. We are getting such concepts now, to be sure, but we associate them with war sacrifices. Could we extend them to sacrifices for the achievement of full employment and all-out production in peace?

10

FACING THE NATIONAL DEBT

LET US RETURN to the world
of 1943, and try to face squarely the matter of the national
debt. Inflation can be held down, if Congress has the courage,
by means of higher taxes, forced savings, adequate price and
wage controls, rationing. But the debt is growing by leaps and
bounds. It will continue to grow so long as we are short of
Utopia—that perfect land where all the war costs are covered by current taxes.

What is to be the end of this huge national war debt?

$250 Billions in 1946?

On the basis of our 1943 estimates, shown in the table on
page 89, the debt will increase by some $60 billions.[1] On
January 1, 1943, the total federal debt was just over $100 bil-
lions, so we can expect $160 by the end of the year. If by
1944 we can match the British tax ratio of 50 per cent of war
costs, we can hold the increase in debt to some $40 billions.
That makes $200 billions by the end of 1944. If the war lasts
through 1945, the total might not exceed $250 billions at the

1. For the fiscal year ending July 1, 1944, President Roosevelt, in his
message to Congress last January, estimated a deficit of $57 billions.

end of that year. At an average rate of 2.5 per cent, this would make the postwar interest burden $6.25 billions a year—larger than the whole federal budget in 1929. On a 2 per cent basis the burden would be $5 billions a year.

Even more serious than the interest burden may be the inflationary effect of the new debt. How many new dollars will be pumped into the system? For 1943 we estimated roughly $30 billions (page 92), a dangerously high proportion. But assuming again that we boost taxes and sales of bonds to the public to the British ratios by 1944, then the new dollars pumped in might be relatively negligible. Assume, for instance, that five billions are injected in 1944, and an equal number in 1945. That would give us on January 1, 1946, 40 billion more dollars in the system than we have today.

At that point we should have a choice of two courses: accept a higher price level after the war, or use taxes to retire some of the dead weight debt and thus cancel out the new dollars. My guess is that we shall accept the higher price level. The London *Economist* guesses the same way:

It seems highly unlikely that after the end of this war we shall revert to the cycles of inflation and deflation which characterised the nineteenth, and the first four decades of the twentieth centuries. The pull of a metallic standard . . . has probably ceased to operate forever. . . . At the close of this war there will be ample inflationary potential to carry further the gradual depreciation of money, and in the immense tasks of reconstruction there will be more than adequate material for harnessing that potential. On the other hand, there will be no . . . conventional monetary criterion to urge us on the road of contraction, retrenchment and deflation.

The monetary history of the world provides . . . one long illustration of the safety valve of currency depreciation easing the load of debt which otherwise would have stifled all economic progress. Given the rate at which national debts are piling up the world over, the need for such indirect alleviations of the real weight of debt will be stronger at the end of this war than in any previous period in history. The task will then be to evolve practical methods of avoiding the disasters to which an over-rapid decline in the value of money has always given rise in the past.[2]

A little postwar inflation may be a good thing in so far as it eases the load of debt. But a runaway inflation has always produced disaster and will again unless it is prevented. There is no doubt that a creeping inflation is in progress now and will continue throughout the war.

On the Concept of Debt

I was born in New England of a sturdy middle-class family, and all my life I have fought against getting into debt. It is an old New England heritage. Only twice have I been in the toils of creditors, both times when I built a house. I got out as fast as I could, at some cost to the living standards of the family. Being in debt gives me a kind of claustrophobia. I do not even buy a car on the installment plan, but insist on waiting until I have accumulated enough numbers.

If anybody ought to quake at a national debt of two hundred and fifty billions on D-Day, it should be I. But one simple mental adjustment keeps my quaking at a minimum. *I have learned not to identify the national debt with my personal debts.* It is not something akin to a mortgage on my house, but something with quite different characteristics. I am so convinced of this that I can sleep soundly even on nights when the debt is going up at $115,000 a minute.

Because two things have the same name, it does not follow that their characteristics are identical. Hitler is a "man," Churchill is a "man"; are their characteristics identical? It is

2. April 19, 1941.

really a problem in semantics. We should be able to think more clearly if the national debt were called something else —say the "national reserve." If people think on the Aristotelian principle of "A is A," "a debt is a debt"; and that all "debts" are bad, they are likely to lie awake worrying about the mortgage from eleven to one A.M., and about the government's credit from one to three. The rest of the night they can devote to worrying about the war debts of our Allies.

One needs only a preliminary course in semantics to break this spurious identification of personal with public debt. $Debt_1$ is not $debt_2$, any more than $Smith_1$ is $Smith_2$. Every type of debt, like every type of man, has different characteristics, and to say that "a debt is a debt" and no more nonsense about it, is as meaningless as to say that "snow is snow." Every skier knows than $snow_1$ is not $snow_2$. His health depends on this knowledge. He can do fine Christie turns on powder snow, and fracture his leg trying to do the same thing on breakable crust.

A little semantic analysis is useful too in making one realize that a given debt cannot be intelligently discussed by itself. It is only half the story. The other half is investment. "Debt" has sad associations, "investment" pleasant ones; yet they are bound together like Siamese twins. There can be no debtor without a corresponding creditor. One does not borrow from the gods, the stars or the mountains. One borrows from some other human being, looking hopefully for a safe place in which to invest his savings, or the savings of others left in his care.

If nobody had any savings, nobody would make any investments. If nobody made any investments, we should enjoy a debtless world. Our dollars get into the system mostly as a result of debt contracted by someone. Bankers are merchants of debt—and by the same token, merchants of investment. Most durable goods are sold "on time," which means one kind of a debt. Margin trading on the stock market would be impossible without facilities for manufacturing debts quickly and easily. Storekeepers could not carry their inventories, farmers could not carry their crops, without borrowing from time to time. Promoters could not organize new businesses without first going into debt. Governments could not build roads or water systems, let alone fight wars, without contracting debts—at least they never have.

The dollar circuit as such is innocent of debt and could function as well without it as the potato economy did; but our actual financial system is packed in every nook and cranny with debt-investment. Capitalism can be defined as the profitable investment of capital—which means a debt for somebody, unless the investment is in corporation stocks, or one's own business.

Thus when people who do not look like communists tell me that we ought to get rid of debt, I stand amazed at such a revolutionary proposal. They are saying in effect that they want to abolish the capitalist system. No debts, no banks, no bonds, no stock markets. Even the Russians have not gone to such lengths.

A financial system is of course conceivable on an "equity" basis, where all investments are in common stocks, and there are no long-term debts at all. Conceivably it might be a better system than what we have. Such a system was tentatively described by Jerome Frank before the TNEC. But what a revolution in thinking and behavior that would require! It would be far more drastic than changing our thoughts about taxation and idle money. On the whole I am for it, but so am I for Mr. H. G. Wells' World State. I do not expect either for some little time.

Let us make a series of statements about the national debt, in an attempt to get all the major characteristics in and so understand it better.

Statement One

The national debt is at the same time an investment by citizens. You have invested in it, I have invested in it, so have your insurance companies, your savings bank, your regular bank, your trust funds, your college endowment funds, your charities. It is the place where our savings have chiefly gone since 1929. On June 30, 1942, 38 per cent of it was held by commercial banks, 17 per cent by purchasers of savings bonds, 17 per cent by life insurance companies and mutual savings banks, 14 per cent by social security and other government trust funds, the balance by miscellaneous organizations. If by some miracle the debt were paid off tomorrow, we should have such a stupendous pool of idle money in the system that the government would be forced to open the subscription books again lest the whole financial structure collapse. The power of the farm bloc would be as nothing compared to the pressure group which would arise if the government proposed suddenly to liquidate its debt. Most creditors do not want it paid off. Where would they find a safer place for their money?

Statement Two

If the national debt is all internal, as ours is, the nation can hardly go bankrupt. The American people are on both sides of the balance sheet. Nations do not hand themselves over to outsiders in settlement of internal debts. Indeed they do not hand themselves over in settlement of external debts. I cannot remember that we did any foreclosing on the assets of Britain, France and Italy when they defaulted on their war loans. The idea of national bankruptcy in the modern world is a verbal bugaboo. The only way a large nation can go bankrupt today is to run out of men or materials. I should like to quote the Finance Minister of Canada on this point:

How can we use such a term as bankrupting the nation to describe a process under which this country [Canada] has doubled its national income in three years, has wiped out unemployment, has multiplied its production of many things, and learned many types of new skills, has expanded and diversified its equipment, has multiplied its government revenue by more than four times, has enabled millions of its citizens to acquire a nest egg for the future, has mobilized its full strength as a producing machine? . . . No country goes bankrupt in that way.[3]

Statement Three

There is no compelling reason why an internal debt should be paid off completely. In fact the United States is said to be the only nation which has so far followed a policy of paying off its debt in a substantial way.[4] The British are still carrying part of their internal debt from the Napoleonic wars. At certain times, when full employment has been reached and inflation threatens, it is advisable to retire some of the debt, but if we retire too much of it, we run into the aforesaid investors, who want their savings in a safe 2 or 3 per cent secur-

3. J. L. Ilsley. Speech reported in *The New York Times,* March 4, 1943.
4. Gaston Jèze, "Public Debt," in the *Encyclopaedia of the Social Sciences,* Macmillan, 1933.

ity. France even went so far as to issue *rentes perpetuelles,*
practically guaranteeing the thrifty Frenchmen who bought
them that their investment would never be disturbed.

Statement Four

If private long-term investment declines, public investment
must increase, or idle savings will cripple the system. This
is axiomatic in an economy such as ours. It works both ways:
if opportunities to invest in private debt or equities increase,
then the public debt can be retired to a like extent. The savers
have another outlet for their funds.

Statement Five

A national debt which is approximately twice the annual
national income can be borne without too much difficulty,
according to British experience. In 1936 the debt of the
United Kingdom was 224 per cent of the national income.[5]
On this basis, if we come out of the war with a national income of $150 billions (at 1943 prices) and can manage to
hold it at that level, a debt of $300 billions could be
sustained. This outside figure, however, should include state
and city indebtedness for fair comparison with England.

Statement Six

The principal of the debt is a less important figure than
the interest charge. A debt of $300 billions at 2 per cent
would be no more difficult to bear than one of $100 billions
at 6 per cent. It is possible, and even respectable, to convert
a public debt to a lower rate of interest. The British did it

5. Paul W. Stewart and Rufus S. Tucker, *The National Debt and Government Credit,* Twentieth Century Fund, 1937, page 8; see also chart, page 99.

with their consols in 1932, and there is no group in the world so financially orthodox as the City of London. The long-term interest rate has been declining for many years. If the government borrowed solely from its own central bank without interest, there need be no interest burden at all.[6] There would be amortization of the principal, and the fundamental prohibition not to pump too many new dollars into the system would still stand. The National Resources Planning Board has said: "Should the day arrive when the carrying charge on the federal debt becomes oppressive, serious thought should be given to the creation by our modern banking and treasury institutions of non-interest-bearing debt."[7]

Statement Seven

The payment of interest by the government does not decrease the nation's purchasing power. True, the government cannot spend this money, but those who receive the interest can. If they do so, the dollar circuit is unaffected. If they hoard it, however, the usual trouble results. For this reason it is most desirable that the public debt be held by investors from all classes of the population. War bonds should be distributed as widely as possible. If they land up in great blocks in the safes of the well to do, then, as the Brookings Institution points out, the problem of idle money immediately arises. There is also the danger of idle money in the case of savings banks, life insurance companies, and other institutional holders of government securities.

Theoretically it is conceivable that those who get the interest pay taxes to an equivalent amount. In such a case, the

6. As pointed out earlier this amounts to the same thing as printing new money.

7. See also Jerry Voorhis, *Out of Debt, Out of Danger*, 1943.

interest "burden" is a pure bookkeeping charge. Mr. X receives $5,000 on his government bonds, and pays $5,000 in income taxes. He could forget the interest he received, if the government would forget the taxes. Practically, however, it does not work out that way. The interest burden can have serious effects on the internal distribution of income—for example, if ownership of government debt becomes concentrated it creates a class of *rentiers* carried on the backs of the productive members of society. But we must never forget that the interest burden is not a financial loss to the nation as a whole.

Statement Eight

Government debt per se is *not* the cause of inflation. If the economy is on part time, an increase in debt cannot cause general inflation until full employment is reached. Then beware! That is why increases in the debt today are inflationary, while in 1934 they were not.

Statement Nine

Broadly speaking, there are three kinds of public debt:

Dead weight debt, for which no useful plant is built. This includes outlays for war, for relief, or for current expenses.

Passive debt, for non-revenue-producing public works, such as public buildings, parks, playgrounds, monuments like the Lincoln Memorial.

Active debt, for revenue-producing public works, such as toll bridges, the TVA, water works, perpetual-yield forest projects.

How Sweden Balances the Budget

The Swedish government uses a form of federal budget which gives validity to these important distinctions. It indicates what must be collected in taxes, to achieve a true balance. Self-liquidating projects in the *active* debt class are kept outside the budget entirely, unless they show losses.

Projects in the *passive* debt are gradually amortized over the life of the asset. Here in the United States, the government, let us say, constructs a new Interior Building during 1940. The cost is $5 millions, and the 1940 budget takes the full load as an expense for the year. But the building is good for at least twenty-five years. The amortization charge, accordingly, is $200,000. In Sweden that figure is all that would get into the 1940 budget. But an equal amount gets into the budget for 1941, 1942, and so on for twenty-five years.

A budget of the Swedish type is "balanced" when taxes are large enough to cover all regular operating expenses, all interest, and *amortization on the passive debt*. Such a budget will inevitably go out of balance in deep depressions, but will show a surplus in prosperous years. It should always balance over a five- to ten-year period. It tells the nation exactly where it stands financially—as the Swedish people have found to their great advantage. It silences outcries about "balancing the budget" based on emotion, ignorance and politics. It makes it clear that new passive investments should not be undertaken unless the government is willing to impose sufficient taxes to cover the annual amortization. There is no magic about the "double budget." In this country, however, it would impose a financial responsibility on Congress and the Administration hitherto unknown.

A Balance Wheel

In times of depression, government debt in the modern economy has become an important stimulator of the dollar circuit, and a factor which helps to keep the debt-investment system going. It was objected to in the past, and with good reason, because money invested in public outlays absorbed capital which could be more usefully employed in private enterprise. Now when private enterprise does not absorb all of our national savings, we must either reduce the volume of savings or find other outlets for them.

A public debt can be a useful instrument of public policy. It can be used for either beneficent or destructive purposes. In some countries it has been abused by irresponsible politicians to depreciate the currency, finance needless wars, build useless public works, ruin the whole *rentier* class. It can be used, as we have seen, to bring a part-time economy up to full employment, to check inflation, to give investors a safe place for their funds, to keep the dollar circuit turning over at the necessary rate.

Once a depression gets under way, says *Business Week*,[8] businessmen have to curtail their operations. If things get worse the state must step in "to save the profit system from the strangulation of its own compulsions." It may seem strange to regard the public debt as a life raft for business, but there is indisputable evidence in the history of the 1930's to support *Business Week's* contention.

"If a democratic society," says Hansen, "does not take bold action to achieve full employment, including use of fiscal policy to the extent necessary, our system of free enterprise is doomed."[9] Fortunately our public financiers must operate in a goldfish bowl. The measure of their competence can be found in a count of the unemployed. When the number of unemployed is gaining, they are doing a bad job; when it is

8. August 16, 1941.   9. *Harper's*, April 1942.

held to a minimum, they are doing a good one. They must be ready to spend, ready to tax, ready to stop spending and pay off the debt, as the count of the unemployed varies. If a democracy is unable to find leaders who can be held to such vigorous action, its future is dark.

I believe that such leaders can be found. I believe that our new schools of public administration are going to help develop them. I believe that we do not have to surrender democracy in order to operate a dollar circuit which does not periodically break down. In the great winds of change which are now upon us, young men to take up the challenge will appear. Necessity is also the mother of leadership.

The editors of *Fortune* are sobered but not frightened by the prospective burden. In the May 1943 issue they too face the national debt:

Administration of a huge debt for decades to come will be an inescapable necessity. And since it is now a well-established fact that movement of the debt up or down has profound effects on the level of economic activity, we look forward to seeing the powerful instrument thus at our disposal used boldly. It must be used to prevent either deflation and waste of productive resources, or inflation and economic disruption, as the needs of any particular future period may indicate. There will be risks, to be sure; but they will be unavoidable in any case. We shall simply have to run them, but we may feel quite certain that the risks of unemployment and depression will be greater still.

The Final War Bill

A national debt of two to three hundred billions on D-Day need not terrify us. Nor is it anything to be laughed off. Three major readjustments must be made:

1. America must give up her proud and unique position as the only nation without a large standing national debt. Any ideas about

paying off $300 billions in short order must be quite finally laid aside.

2. We must accept taxes high enough to cover the interest charges, always remembering that a large part of the taxes come from those who receive a large part of the interest.

3. We must use the tax structure and the debt, if necessary, to keep the national income high. If national income falls precipitately, the debt will presently become unmanageable. Our economy is now geared to a national output in goods and services of around $150 billions a year. We are like a flying fortress which must maintain a given speed or crash.

We shall probably have to look forward to high tax rates for many years after the war. Some reduction after D-Day will make us feel better, but even then the rates will make 1940 look like Mt. Washington alongside of Everest.

Financial bankruptcy as a result of war outlays is quite impossible. Can we therefore feel not too disturbed about the cost of this war? About the financial cost I think we may. But not about the physical cost. The real war bill is being paid in other currency than dollars, and is being paid now. Much of it will be paid in depleted natural resources. The last war left the legacy of the dust bowl. This one may leave great areas of eroded farmland, priceless forests stripped, mines and oil wells exhausted. We have little time now to think about this physical bill.

There is still another bill, which we dare not think of too much—the cost in dead and disabled men. This will be the highest bill of all. It makes the dollar cost seem trivial and shadowy.

11

WHEN WAR SPENDING STOPS

THE GUNS ARE SILENCED. The far-flung armies of America can come home, except for a skeleton police force. War workers by the millions lay down their tools.

A voice from Washington comes over the radio. It is cleared through every station, beamed to every continent. It reaches every army camp, and every American ship around the seven seas:

You will hear many words of congratulations on your magnificent achievements. The most eloquent words will be inadequate. At this moment I think something more practical is on your minds.

You want to know how we can carry on. You want to know how you can pick up the threads of normal life again. I will tell you.

We could print money and it would keep you going for a few months. Then we could print some more. Before the first lot was spent, however, you would be able to buy only half as much with it. Soon it would be practically worthless—just so much stamped wastepaper.

There is only one way to make it good. You yourselves must make the things which you are going to buy. Unless you produce them, the money is issued against nothing.

Businessmen can employ some of you right away, those whose plants have not been converted to war. Go to your nearest United

States Employment Bureau for information. When other plants are reconverted to peace, businessmen can employ millions more.

But you cannot wait for these jobs. So we have prepared others for you—useful public works and services. The authorities in your own town and state will administer most of the work. Your draft boards and ration boards will help. They will give you advice about retraining programs. The largest project in your community is probably for building new houses. But there are many other projects, calling for every type of skill. The federal government will arrange for the financing. Taxes will not come down much, until the demobilization is bridged. The national debt will be held in line. Prices will not get out of hand. We still have war machinery to take care of that. It is now a war against depression and unemployment.

You can win it, as you have won on the battlefield. But we must all hold our ranks and our discipline. . . . No panic, no pushing, no relaxing. This is perhaps the greatest test of our stamina as a nation.

Your government, of whatever political party, hereby promises to see to it that money is kept in circulation at a rate which results in substantially full employment. If businessmen cannot do it all, as they cannot today with their plants in process of conversion, we will supplement them, and go on doing it.

You have not fought this war for the privilege of selling apples on street corners. Soldiers, you will have work. Businessmen, you will have orders. Consumers—which means everyone—you will receive the essential goods you need. More and more goods as we hold our ranks. Allies, you will continue to get food and necessary supplies.

Courage, then, and we will see it through together!

Boom or Collapse?

Some such message from Uncle Sam will be in order on Demobilization Day, with specific plans to back it.

In Chapter 2 we predicted that the American economy will look like something from back of the moon when D-Day comes. This is not entirely a disturbing prospect. It implies that our minds will be well-ventilated for change. The folkways will be in flux, and we can face things, plan things, execute things, which would not have been possible in 1940. The great financial fears—soon to be discussed—will be temporarily forgotten under the sheer pressure of events. What are the prospects for achieving stability and then genuine prosperity after the armistice? Can the voice from Washington make good?

Most economists today are predicting a great boom when peace arrives. They reason that citizens will have plenty of money, and war bonds which they can cash, combined with a huge shopping list of postponed purchases. Citizens, they say, will descend upon the market to bid up prices for cars, washing machines, coffee and silk stockings. Unemployment will develop later, when the buying spree has subsided. These economists point to the inflationary boom after the last war, followed by a slump to six million unemployed in 1921.

This prediction sounds logical, but I do not believe that it covers all the pertinent factors. It is dangerous to draw conclusions based on the last war, where we got in only to our knees, with 25 per cent of national effort involved. This time we shall be up to our necks, with perhaps 70 per cent of the national effort devoted to battle. Again, deferred demand for consumers' goods does not guarantee a boom. No matter how much loose change citizens can lay their hands on, if they are *afraid of the future* they will hesitate to spend it. They will save their money as a cushion for hard times. Businessmen will not branch out if they are afraid. Fear of depression can help bring depression by slowing down the spending rate. If people are alarmed at the prospects for the long swing, they will not throw their money around much in the demobilization period.

D-Day in 1918

The rosy picture of 1919, as a painless demobilization and swift removal of government controls, does not quite square with history. The demobilization of the armed forces, including a $60 bonus for every soldier, required large government expenditures. Many war projects were completed after the war ended. Fifteen hundred ships were delivered *after* the Armistice, against 500 before it. Many contracts for munitions could not be canceled, and damages were paid by the government for a number of those that were canceled.

After November 11, 1918, we loaned two billion dollars to our Allies, practically all of which was spent inside this country. Treasury spending in 1919 was actually greater than in 1917; in the early months of 1919 it was still running as high as in 1918. Our excess of exports over imports reached its high point in 1919—largely food and cotton going to cold and hungry Europe. A large flow of private investment went at once into new mass-production industries, and this, combined with large government expenditures, cushioned the demobilization period. As European fields and factories began to come back into production in 1920, our exports were hit a terrific blow. The farmers' boom collapsed—and stayed collapsed for twenty years.

Production of automobiles for civilians was not cut by government order until March 1918, and then only by 30 per cent. Other industrial cuts went into effect in September 1918, two months before Armistice Day. They were thus too late to cause any material diversion of output to munitions.

The industries affected included bicycles, heating appliances, boilers, refrigerators, sewing machines, stoves, tires, pianos. Reduced staffs were held, ready to swing back as soon as peace came, and they had not long to wait.

Reconversion After This War

Today, on the contrary, many great industries have been almost wholly converted to war—automobiles, refrigerators, washing machines, metal furniture, vacuum cleaners, phonographs, lighting fixtures, oil burners, typewriters, radios. A friend of mine who produces radio equipment cannot get materials to make even replacement parts for civilian sets. It will require a complete retooling job to reconvert most of these industries. Retooling is a time-consuming process, and calls for only a few skilled mechanics while it is going on. Remember the minor depression while Ford retooled for Model A in 1927. That job took him the better part of a year. Some estimates for new automobile models after this war have allowed for a conversion period of eighteen months. Redvers Opie, economic adviser to the British Embassy, reports that certain British industries now estimate that it may take them three years to reconvert.[1] Recent estimates for the United States, however, are more reassuring: radio, two to three months; refrigerators and other major electrical appliances, four to six months; automobiles, five to nine months. After all, conversion from war to peace should not take longer than from peace to war.

Selling organizations today are being ruthlessly broken up. Staffs for quick peacetime production are not being maintained as in 1918. Meanwhile the normal markets of 1940

1. *The New York Times,* February 26, 1943.

have been torn to pieces by government price-fixing, rationing, standardization, and above all by selling a converted output to a single buyer, the government. Vast areas of business relationships will have to be re-established from the ground up, including the thorny question of what to do with war plants built by the government and leased to private concerns.

Clifford J. Durr, of the Federal Communications Commission, gives a striking picture of how war has twisted normal business relationships. He told the annual meeting of the American Economic Association in January 1943:

> We see in operation a new kind of profit system which is not capitalism, and a new kind of private enterprise which is not based on private initiative. It is a system in which the government provides the capital and takes the financial risk, while business is paid a management fee for the hire of its organization, and in which the manufacturer furnishes the technical skill, ingenuity and organizing ability. The government provides the market and says what and how much is to be produced.

The whole element of risk, along with both the rewards and the punishments attendant upon risk-taking, has been largely banished for the duration. If the duration is long, will businessmen have forgotten how to get out and scramble for business? They are scrambling now to get out production, and an excellent job they are doing. What will be their psychological attitude—say in 1946—when they must turn from making things to selling things?

The Problem of Expansion

The last war took place in an environment which was still tuned to expansion from natural causes. Population was increasing rapidly; there was confidence in investment outlets; many of the great monopolies of today were only in embryo;

progress was believed to be inevitable. Progress was not inevitable, as we have since learned, but the *belief* was there. Manufacturers were not much worried about excess capacity, and nobody ever mentioned a "mature economy."

The present environment, on the contrary, follows a decade of depression and stagnation; a decade to which only the disaster of war was able to bring full employment. Businessmen fought bitterly against expanding their plants in 1941 because of fear of too much capacity after the war. They issued one solemn report after another saying that we had enough steel capacity, railroad capacity, aluminum capacity, power capacity, for every need. They have patriotically expanded since then, but it would be premature to say that they have stopped worrying.

While there may be a great new market in the field of light metals and plastics, much of it will be *at the expense of older materials*. Aluminum, magnesium and plywood will replace steel and copper in many articles. Such replacement is not expansion but competition, and thus not all velvet by any means.

Indeed, with many billions of dollars of new plant and equipment added by war, it is hard to see the need for plant expansion in many lines, beyond the necessary outlays for conversion. If we end the war with a national income of $150 billions (at 1943 prices), that may mean at least $20 billions of annual savings. How will private industry be able immediately to absorb any such sum?

The Psychology of Demand

Undoubtedly there will be a large postwar demand for durable consumers' goods, especially automobiles. But what if there are no such goods to be had until retooling is complete? The demand alone cannot create much employment until there are goods to buy. We may have an interval of totally empty shelves for many products.

It is often assumed that the demand for goods is cumulative; that we shall want all the stuff we have foregone during the war. This assumption is untrue. Demand does not keep, any more than fish. Reduced consumption of "soft" goods— food and the like—is gone forever, while reduced consumption of durable goods is *not* mathematically cumulative. Take your own experience. You used to buy a new car every year, let us say. Suppose the war lasts four years. Will you replace your old car with four new ones? Hardly. The other three are gone forever, together with the second cups of coffee you would have liked but never got.

Again, suppose the automobile companies, in order to cut the retooling period, take the canvas off their old dies and go back to 1942 models. There is talk of their doing just this. It looks as if it would help the unemployment situation. Will it? Will you buy a 1942 Ford in 1946, when you have long since been sold on a brand new plastic job, 50-miles-to-the-gallon? Or will you drive your old crate while it still has the strength to run out of the garage? I am going to wait until I can get one of those dream boats that I see in the four-color ads. I think most Americans will wait too, even if it means a year instead of four months. We shall be used to waiting by 1946. How far will this habit of waiting apply to other durable goods, like refrigerators, radios, washing machines?

"Normalcy" Again?

As in 1919, we shall be called on for enormous exports to

the rest of the world, and this will provide a market for the food industries, and for various kinds of equipment and drugs. These shipments will hardly be privately financed, but will be a continuation of lend-lease. No hasty retreat to "normalcy" is indicated here.

Ever since the war began, one committee after another has been trying to do something about the little businessman. Millions of tender words have been expended on his behalf. But the committees make small progress. Day by day big business gains at the expense of little business. The blunt truth is that war production can be handled more easily through big units. Harassed War Department executives are going to deal with big units whenever and wherever they can. Total war is not a respecter of worthy causes, whether they be Federal Arts Projects or patriotic little businessmen. D-Day will find the role of big business greatly expanded over 1940, which means that the area of administered or rigid prices will gain heavily as against the area of free competition. Small business, furthermore, will have lost a great number of its young, energetic men to the armed services—the men who would otherwise be pushing ahead in competitive markets.

Our economy, accordingly, will come out of the war even less flexible than it went in. If government controls are severed on D-Day and everything left to "the market," and if we are right that this market will be stiff in the joints, should we not fairly expect the adjustment to be exceptionally difficult?

If we are making $100 billions (at 1943 prices) of war goods on D-Day, and $50 billions of civilian goods, and aim to hold the national income at around $150 billions, the shift is obviously gigantic. It will not be a shift of $100 billions, because much war production will continue, together with lend-lease, while public works and services will fill some of the gulf. We might, however, reverse the figures during the demobilization period—ending with $100 billions of civilian goods at a rough guess, and $50 billions for military, lend-lease and public works outlays.

Ghost Towns

In the light of these more or less brutal considerations, I find it difficult to anticipate a roaring boom at D-Day, especially if all government controls are severed. It did not happen that way even in 1919. We might indeed get some roaring prices for those goods still on the shelves, but with all controls abandoned we should certainly get wholesale unemployment at the same time. The situation in war boom areas, like Detroit, Seattle and Bridgeport, might become revolutionary.

Michigan will confront the worst unemployment in its history, according to Governor Harry F. Kelly. That is saying a good deal, for Detroit has had some shattering crises. It was there that the bank closing spiral of 1932-1933 began. The governor estimates that 400,000 people will be looking for work as the automotive and aircraft industries go out of war production.

In the war boom towns like Detroit there will simply not be jobs enough even after retooling is complete. Innumerable workers will have to get out of Detroit, and out of many other areas. To date we have "no well developed mechanisms to deal with geographical displacements, including the transportation of workers and their families."[2]

2. A. F. Hinrichs in *Survey Graphic,* May 1943. An excellent article on the demobilization problem.

What the People Want

The American people seem to sense this critical situation. The National Association of Manufacturers employed the Psychological Corporation to conduct a survey on the question.[3] The results were emphatic. "Ninety-two per cent of persons representing all wage groups were in favor of immediate planning for the postwar era rather than waiting until the war is won. Six per cent were opposed, two per cent undecided. Sixty-one per cent were in favor of the immediate preparation of a vast public works program; 24 per cent were opposed, the balance undecided. But 80 per cent were opposed to government operation of private business."

The people want plans developed now for full employment. They want the government to fill any gaps, but not to take over private industry. There are bound to be gaps which businessmen cannot fill. Such fissures have been open indeed since the last war. Highway and school building accounted for millions of jobs in the prosperous twenties, as we have seen. Throughout the thirties, private business came nowhere near employing all our people. Only by the most strenuous wishful thinking can one believe that this record will be suddenly set aside on D-Day—particularly when we remember the great increase in laborsaving methods which the war is developing.

New Laborsaving Devices

I talked recently to a worker in one of our great industrial companies, now converted 100 per cent to war. He is a member of the enterprising labor-management committee which the WPB has helped to establish in the plant. He is doing

3. *The New York Times*, February 14, 1943.

everything he can to stimulate production and win the war, but being something of a philosopher he cannot help wondering where it is all going to end up.

"Why, we're making improvements around this shop that would knock your eye out! Thirty per cent increase in output per man-hour on that bunch of lathes, 20 per cent in this whole department. A brand new method for repairing dies, invented by a worker—that redheaded guy over in the corner. It's swell for winning the war. What is it going to do to employment around here when the war is over?"

"You tell me," I said.

His lips closed in a grim line. "It's going to raise hell, that's what it's going to do. It may put half of us on the street as compared with the same output before the war. But I'm telling you, we're not going to stay on the street. We're not going to stand for another ten, twenty years of depression. If the country can go all out for war and hire everybody, it can go all out for peace. If industry can't do the job, the answer is public works, and I don't mean raking leaves."

Colonel Lewis Sanders, testifying before a Congressional committee in February 1943, said that industrial engineers have cut the production time on a medium bomber from 70,000 man-hours to 13,000, and on a 10,000-ton Liberty cargo ship from 1,100,000 man-hours to 680,000. This gives a hint of the revolution in laborsaving devices now under way. A much broader hint is found in a report of the Department of Commerce, issued in April 1943. Department statisticians calculate that if our output after the war is no greater than it was in 1940, there will be more than nineteen million unemployed. They figure that the country will be in a position to produce almost 50 per cent more goods and services than in the best prewar years. Shall we be wise enough to consume them without depending on war or disaster?

Postwar Timing

If D-Day comes by 1946, the physical structure of the American economy should be the strongest in its history, as we noted in Chapter 3. Plant, raw materials, skilled workers, should be available for a vast increase in living standards. But business-as-usual will be so changed and twisted by war, that it looks as if only the most carefully planned program would enable the strong physical structure to assert itself. Simply to relax all controls and allow nature to take its course, would appear to be an infallible recipe for calamity.

Citizens will have plenty of money available when the war ends, but they will not spend it if they are afraid. They will spend if they are assured of a margin of security, and a peacetime job coming along in due course. This calls for timing as carefully prepared as the program for landing our troops in French Africa. The details will require exhaustive research, but the timing might follow some such order as this:

1. Begin planning now, at once, for both the short swing and long swing periods. Plan for two periods of demobilization, after fighting ends in Europe and in the Far East. Government men, businessmen, labor leaders, should work together on the programs. Arrange the terms for canceling war contracts, for stock piles, for ships and aircraft for future use.

2. Give these plans reasonable publicity. Do not promise too much, but start building up public confidence.

For the Short Swing

3. When the fighting stops, taper off war spending. At the same time, initiate public works and a program of social security which

guarantees all Americans a minimum living standard. Provide a dismissal wage for war workers.

4. Hold the war controls against inflation, and hold tax rates at a high level.

5. Help businessmen, technically and financially, to reconvert their plants. Encourage them to take as much responsibility for employment as they can. Tax allowances may be in order. Offer smaller firms a chance to buy some of the new government plants now operated by large corporations.

6. Aim at full employment. As it is approached, taper off public works, but hold social security. Taper off whatever war controls have been retained for the emergency.

For the Long Swing

7. Extend social security. Promote higher living standards for all. Inaugurate automatic controls for full employment on the principles of a "compensatory economy"—shortly to be discussed. Seek an international balance of exports and imports to supplant lend-lease. The Santa Claus role has its limits.

8. When stability seems assured, pay off some of the dead-weight war debt.

Controls to Drop and to Hold

When the war ends we shall be tied up in more controls than a jumper tangled in a parachute. If we cut the entire network, we shall be quite free—to crash. Are there any controls which can be safely cut or loosened to let us down easier?

I think that we could soon get rid of gas rationing, unless tires were still unobtainable. That would give us a few deep breaths and help the roadside industries. Sugar rationing will be eased as the Caribbean opens to peacetime traffic.

House construction can begin, with controls relaxed on metals, lumber, hardware, coal, power; but plumbing and heating fixtures may be delayed. Dimouts and blackouts will end, and the long vigils of airplane spotters. Colleges and schools can go back to normal semesters—though one wonders if the curriculum will ever be the same again.[4] Taxes on luxuries can soon come down, and other nuisance taxes. Manpower controls can be greatly eased. No more forced savings. No more censorship. Installment credit restrictions can be loosened.

What controls must stay? Primarily the financial ones. Price fixing and rationing must be continued to guard against inflation, to insure equality in the distribution of scarce essential goods, and to help war victims abroad. Rent controls should stay until the housing program really opens up.

Contracts for war materials should be eased off, not severed sharply. If they are for things which have peacetime uses—such as ships, or foods or medicines—it might be sound policy to complete the contracts.

Above all, the armed services must not be demobilized faster than the community has the power to absorb them. Undersecretary of War Robert P. Patterson has an important suggestion in this connection:[5]

The War Department will help develop a method of *reversing* the action of Selective Service. Through Selective Service the men were brought to this job. When peace comes, it should bring the job to them. That's the way to keep a firm social and economic system. That's the way to discharge the obligation this nation is under.

4. How about offering men discharged from the armed services a technical furlough, with full pay, until they finish college, if they desire to accept it? This would not cover their college expenses, but would provide a helpful scholarship. How much better than a cash bonus!

5. Speaking at Northwestern University, Chicago, January 24, 1943.

12

A COMPENSATORY ECONOMY

W<small>ELL, **WHERE DOES THE MONEY**</small>
come from? Where did Russia, Italy, Japan, Germany get
the money for their vast military and building programs?
Where did Britain and America get it for their colossal war
outlays? They got most of it out of the labor of people and
machines hitherto underemployed. In the world after the
war, enormous quotas of labor and plant will be withdrawn
from lethal activities. They can be monetized again, as in the
war, but this time for the production of wealth.

Will these factories and workers be put to useful postwar
work? They certainly will be in Russia. They probably will
be in Britain, Canada, Australia. They can be here. The London *Economist* believes that the machinery to do the task is
already available in the financial structure. The Treasury, the
central bank, the commercial banks, the methods for issuing
check money and currency, do not need to be revolutionized.
They only need to be aimed in the right direction, and
operated by men with intelligence and courage.

The real discovery of wartime is not that finance in itself is hum-
bug, but that finance is only a means to an end. The end is the distribution of the nation's income in such a way as, on the one hand,

to secure a maximum output of goods and services from the physical resources available, and, on the other hand, to insure a minimum of necessities for every individual and family in the community. . . . The role of finance is merely to make certain, by its influence on the distribution of the national income between different claimants, that financial considerations are never an obstacle to programs which are physically possible. . . . It should be possible to work out from statistical knowledge of the real national income, and its optimum distribution between investment and consumption, a policy of full employment.[1]

It is not necessary to go out and find some money in order to put people to work; it is necessary to put people to work in order that modern money can be placed in circulation. William T. Foster put it neatly when he said: "Americans did not ride around in 25 million automobiles because they were prosperous—but were prosperous because they rode around in 25 million automobiles."

Power of a Nation

The question of where's the money coming from has one answer in the case of the individual, and quite a different answer in the case of all individuals united in a nation. As in the matter of debt, it is meaningless to identify the individual with the nation as a whole. That kind of thinking leads into a blind alley. If you have no money, you cannot buy that beautiful new car. Period. But if you, and all your fellow citizens, want to buy a beautiful new river development project or a beautiful new war, there is nothing to stop you from doing so. What you can "afford" moves into an entirely new dimension.

1. Leading editorial, "The Financial Instrument," London *Economist*, December 19, 1942.

In your collective capacity you can put men and machines hitherto idle to work. When this pool is exhausted, you can transfer man power from making cars to making tanks. You can issue claim checks for the new war production, and then tax them back or borrow them back in a closed circuit—as we noted in Chapter 9. You can buy your war and its costly equipment right up to the limit of the nation's man power, machine-hours and materials. There will be no difficulty about the money—as there is none today in any belligerent nation.

A rough analogy for the individual would be a situation where you wanted a car, had no money, but had some time to spare. By working in that spare time your labor could be monetized and presently you would have the cash to buy the car. Actually you cannot often do this because of the lack of infallible opportunities for spare time jobs, particularly if there is much unemployment about. But a nation acting through its government always can. It makes the new jobs through its orders for guns, bombers and machine tools, irrespective of "market" conditions. The more unemployment there is about, the more jobs it can make. The money follows the work, and the taxes follow the money.

Except for our fears and financial traditions, the same formula can be followed in peacetime. The orders then, however, are for highways, schools and Grand Coulees, or for food, shelter and clothing purchased by those who receive social security benefits. So long as there is slack in the economy, you and your fellow citizens acting through your government can always take it up, by expanding the orders on industry in peace or in war. But you must take it up deliberately and with forethought. The slack will not take itself up in any world that we can now see ahead of us.

Four Roads to Full Employment

Theoretically, full employment can be achieved in four ways:

1. By a completely rationed economy in which citizens are assigned to work, as in an army, and then go to the mess hall and get their supplies. Money is not used at all.

2. By a completely socialized economy where the state owns all the industrial and agricultural plant, and appoints managers to operate it. Money is used, consumers have some free choices, but the government runs everything, and free enterprise disappears.

3. By a mixed or compensatory economy, where businessmen largely own and operate the means of production, but where the government underwrites full employment by its control of existing financial machinery—as the *Economist* suggests.

4. By a free competitive economy, where savings are so promptly invested that the dollar circuit is always closed, and plant and labor resources are always fully used. This condition was approached by some countries for certain periods in the nineteenth century, but for the last generation every nation has been getting farther away from it. It is unworkable if opportunities for investment fail to keep pace with savings. It is unworkable if prices are taken out of the free market and controlled by corporate groups, monopolies, trade associations, or labor unions. Both things have happened since 1914, in such a big way that only the most starry-eyed dreamer can look for the complete re-establishment of free competition. It is like looking for the re-establishment of the medieval guilds.[2]

In poll after poll the American people have rejected by large majorities various proposals for rationed and socialized economies, and in poll after poll they have demanded, by even larger majorities, full employment after the war.[3] If full employment is denied them, their opposition to more radical proposals is likely to wither rapidly. Some very

2. Radical theorists who called themselves Guild Socialists used to dream about this in the 1920's.

3. See article by Elmo Roper, *Survey Graphic*, May 1943.

radical methods indeed won popular acceptance in Europe. People in the mass are not interested in theories, they are interested in results. They prefer bread and work, whatever the social theory, to no bread on the loftiest ideological grounds.

Principles of a Compensatory Economy

A compensatory economy—method number 3 above—offers a working compromise between "present principles" and totalitarian rigors. The state is the underwriter, not the operator. *Fortune,* in its Supplement of December 1942, develops the thesis that the choice is no longer between free competition and more or less rigorous forms of state control, but between the state as financial underwriter and the state as production manager; between planning at strategic points and an all-out planned economy. With the state as underwriter, a large area of free enterprise can be maintained, perhaps expanded. *Fortune* bows to the compulsions of history: "Today the government is governing an industrial society, and the condition of private industry must be one of its primary concerns."

We can recognize four basic principles in a compensatory economy:

First, businessmen should carry the maximum possible load of production and distribution, so long as the output is sound, in demand, and able to pay its way.

Second, the federal government, in co-operation with local governments and local groups, undertakes to fill any serious gaps in employment left vacant by ordinary business activity. This is done chiefly by financing local projects, not by direct federal construction. Taxation and government investment are the primary levers.

Third, the federal government insures national minimum standards, by social security legislation, and by public works and services in the fields of health, housing, nutrition, education.

Fourth, government benefits should be extended primarily to citizens as *consumers,* rather than to producer groups. Subsidies to keep inefficient businesses afloat—no matter how small and pathetic they may seem, subsidies to farm blocs, subsidies to labor organizations, are not contemplated in this plan. Subsidies to children, mothers, old people, sick people, people temporarily unemployed, are. This principle will undoubtedly be assailed by pressure groups, but I am nailing it to the masthead right here. Says E. H. Carr:

The housing subsidies of the past brought prosperity to the building trade . . . the distribution of cheap milk assures the milk producer of a regular market. In short, to subsidize consumption is almost always the soundest way of helping production.[4]

Consumers First

Dr. J. Frederic Dewhurst, Economist of the Twentieth Century Fund, reinforces the point.[5] He is against producers' subsidies, because he feels that they destroy the benefits of competition. If consumers have adequate purchasing power they create a market for which producers can compete. If the product is too dear, or of poor quality, producers must improve it or be eliminated. But the individual producer, being also a consumer, would be protected in a compensatory economy against the loss of the necessities of life for himself and his family. He cannot fall into the cellar, but only to the ground floor, from which he can try again.

4. E. H. Carr, *Conditions of Peace,* Macmillan, 1942.
5. In conversations with the author.

Dr. Dewhurst is suspicious of subsidies given to producers' organizations just to keep them alive or to "make work." Let them die and let their promoters get into something which is really wanted. If the war is to develop light metals for consumers, should the nation subsidize the steel industry at its old rate of production? It should not. It did not subsidize carriage makers when the automobile came in. A monopoly is often a scheme to subsidize an industry to perpetuity and keep out competitors who have cheaper, better products. Producers should be kept on their toes or they should be wiped out, says Dr. Dewhurst. Stuffing them with sugar is bad for the economy and bad for them. It is up to free enterprisers to show some enterprise. Some subsidies to producers may be necessary in the demobilization period, but not for the long-swing reconstruction.

A Measuring Rod

The first technique needed to carry out the principles of a compensatory economy is a way of measuring its health and well-being. The simplest measuring rod is one suggested earlier—a count of the unemployed. The United States has never done this completely and regularly, but other nations have, including Britain, Germany and Sweden. A nonpolitical research staff, perhaps in some university, should be empowered to give the government and the people careful monthly figures on those seeking work.

A statistical measure of this kind, combined with routine controls which would operate automatically when the figures reach a given level, would afford real protection against political abuses. Its action would not be political, but would be similar to the thermostat control on your furnace, or to the chemical controls which keep the human body in delicate equilibrium.

Dr. Cannon of Harvard, a distinguished physiologist, has described these automatic chemical controls, and pointed out how something of the sort might be devised for social situations, if and when scientific intelligence comes to be applied to economic matters. "It is noteworthy," he writes, "that in the bodily organism such powers as storing or releasing material reserves, hastening or checking continuous processes, are exercised not by the cerebral cortex . . . but by lower centers of the brain which work in an automatic manner when appropriate signals call them to act."[6]

Having established a count of the unemployed, the government should install the routine controls. It should set a standard, close to full capacity, below which employment should never be permitted to fall. The figure for unemployment would probably be somewhere between two and three million persons. In 1929, we had perhaps two million in the "frictional" class, moving from job to job. The measuring rod of unemployment would tell the people regularly how well the dollar circuit is performing, and when the government should step in—or out. No political oratory could obscure the figure.

Another useful yardstick would be the rate of spending for consumers' goods. Say the optimum rate—that at which resources are fully employed—is $10 billions of consumer spending a month. When the index drops to $9 billions, action should at once be taken to increase it. If it rises to $11 billions, action in the reverse direction would be in order, to avert inflation. At present we have no reliable figures for the rate of spending.

6. Walter B. Cannon, *The Wisdom of the Body*, Norton, 1932.

The Taxation Lever

The purpose of these yardsticks or thermostats is to keep the dollar circuit turning at an even rate. Idle money must not impede the flow; hot money must not speed it up. How can the rate be controlled? Chiefly through the federal tax structure.

I do not propose, with my present knowledge, or in the present space, to prepare a blueprint of a tax machine which will meet all requirements. As I write, the country is convulsed with its efforts to produce a satisfactory tax to finance the war. What the post-armistice tax model will look like I do not know—except that it will be derived directly from war experience. Modern inventions do not spring fully armed from the head of Jove; they stand on one another's shoulders.

All I propose to do in this book is to speculate about various tax models, either in operation or around the corner, and to insist as forcefully as I can that a compensatory economy requires a flexible and efficient tax engine to make it go. By means of such an engine, idle money can be kept from accumulating in the system. By means of it social security benefits are paid for, and public works financed—unless they pay their own way, like a toll bridge. By means of it an inflationary boom can be stopped in its tracks, the national debt can be kept within bounds, the budget balanced over reasonable periods, and businessmen assured of dependable markets.

Our tax structure to date, 1943, has not been designed at all; it is a rickety, creaking hulk. It should be remodeled and streamlined from stem to stern. First, the tax system should be based squarely on ability to pay; second, it should be simplified—perhaps to the extent of one collecting agency for the nation, which then distributes the proceeds to federal,

state and local governments according to percentages fixed
by law. The forms themselves should be simplified, at least
to the point where it does not take a firm of C.P.A.'s to understand them.

Many students believe that the income tax is the fairest
method of promoting the public policies we have in mind.
It is superbly fair in that if you have no income you pay no
tax—in contrast with sales taxes which can take away the essentials of life from the poor, and property taxes which you
are supposed to pay even if you have no income. Taxes on
inheritances are also fair in principle, and socially useful in
breaking up swollen fortunes.

An income tax will be paid by at least forty million Americans in 1943. Before the war four million was the maximum.
This broadening of the tax base will be of inestimable value
in postwar finance. The man on the street will get used to it,
as he has in England. Hitherto Congress has been cowardly
in laying direct taxation. "Fearing to face the realities of the
personal income tax, we pick up pennies out of drug stores,
and nickels at the door of movies."[7]

A Tax on Idle Money

A graduated income tax, with higher rates in the upper
brackets, is one way to keep money moving. It may not, however, be the best way. Certainly it tends to discourage venture
capital, and puts a premium on investment in tax-exempt
securities. What other methods should be considered? The
government might collect a direct tax on money, to make it
move. Various students in the last quarter century have advocated such a direct tax, in one form or another. Among

7. David Cushman Coyle, *Roads to a New America,* Little, Brown, 1938.

them are Arthur Dahlberg, Irving Fisher, Silvio Gesell, Ralph W. Manuel, C. William Hazelett, and many others. Mr. Dahlberg has explained the need for taxing money directly. He says:[8]

> Sooner or later we must boldly face the question whether society can function within limits which people tolerate when it maintains rules which
>
> (1) enable money savings to be made predominantly by those people whose personal needs do not induce them to disburse the savings;
>
> (2) then permit hoarding privileges to the holders of money which enable them to defer their disbursements indefinitely; and
>
> (3) automatically generate depression and hardship if the money savings are disbursed more slowly than they are received.
>
> Our present rules seem not to constitute a well-integrated machine.

Indeed they do not, as this book keeps saying from many angles. The machine gets clogged with cash, the way spring mud in Russia clogs a tank. Mr. Dahlberg proposes a de-clogging device which would make it unprofitable and un-comfortable to accumulate large idle bank accounts. He pro-poses a federal tax on bank deposits, together with an in-genious plan to prevent their flight into currency when the tax date comes around. The State of Illinois now collects a tax on deposits once a year, but the depositor can easily evade it by transferring his account temporarily to another bank out-side the state. Only a nation-wide federal tax could prevent this.

Mr. Dahlberg would collect a federal tax on demand bank deposits which show an average monthly balance of $5,000 or more. In order to break us in to the idea without too much pain, he would begin slowly, then gradually increase the

8. TNEC Monograph No. 25.

rate, from say one per cent the first year to a maximum of perhaps 4 per cent. The rate would be set at the figure which made the money move.

If you had $10,000 in the bank cooling its heels, and were faced with a tax of $300 or $400 on it, what would you do? You would spend or invest enough of it to bring the balance below the taxable level; in this case you would hustle around to spend or invest at least $5,000. Mr. Dahlberg believes that the tax would force hoarded money into three channels:

1. To the capital goods industries on lower terms than before. This would stimulate businessmen to expand their plant.

2. To the durable goods field, again at such low terms "that almost unlimited housing activity, for example, would result."

3. To consumers for installment purchases. You could get a car or a refrigerator on time for less money, and the standard of living of consumer-borrowers could be substantially raised.

In brief, "from the social point of view, a tax on money would simply impel people into demanding goods, into producing goods, and into creating and obtaining new dollars which correspond to the new goods." Mr. Dahlberg believes that he has developed a foolproof social invention, and various experts agree with him. This is not the place either to advocate the plan or to describe its various complicated details. You can find them in the TNEC monograph quoted above. Here we are simply looking at ideas for taxing idle money into active motion. Sooner or later one of these ideas is going to hit Congress and the nation with as much urgency and excitement as the Ruml plan for tax reform hit us in the spring of 1943.

If you are dubious about Mr. Dahlberg's proposal, Professor Irving Fisher can give you another one with a similar objective, based not on outright taxes but on money which depreciates through time. The longer you hold it, the less its value becomes.[9]

If you are dubious about dated money—and I confess that I am—let us take a look at C. William Hazelett's "incentive taxation." Mr. Hazelett is a distinguished inventor with many industrial developments to his credit. Lately he has been giving most of his time to a social invention for taxing idle money. He believes, rightly I think, that until we bring our financial system up to date, the outlook for mechanical inventors is precarious.[10]

In testimony before the Senate Finance Committee in August 1942, Mr. Hazelett summarized the 1942 revenue bill in these unkind words: "You have in a 320-page document the most complicated and controversial tax bill in history. It will bring no fraction of the revenue required. It will penalize and restrict production, which will determine the outcome of the war."

The Senators asked what he had to offer as an alternative. He gave it to them in a one-page tax bill which he declared could "bring all the revenue that can be collected, which will stimulate instead of restrict production, and which will be acceptable to your constituents as entirely just."

The bill first imposed a tax on idle money. "All individuals and corporations having average cash balances in excess of $300, shall pay two per cent of said balance for each turnover less than 8. If turnover exceeds 8 per year, the tax is nothing." Cash balances include both currency and bank money. The second part of the bill proposed a tax on spendings.

Unless the taxpayer keeps his money turning over fast

9. See his book *Stamp Scrip*, Adelphi, New York, 1933.
10. See Mr. Hazelett's book, *A Dynamic Capitalism*, Harper, 1943.

enough, Mr. Hazelett wants him to be taxed smartly and progressively. The slower the cash balance moves, the heavier the tax. "Moving" is defined as any kind of spending, or investment or contribution, which puts people to work—buying food, building a house, subscribing for war bonds, investing in a new oil field, writing a check to the Red Cross.

The tax would apply to corporations as well as to individuals, and is indeed proposed as the *only* federal tax on corporations. Mr. Hazelett's idea is that when a company puts its money promptly to work by raising wages, enlarging the plant or declaring dividends, it should pay no tax at all. But whenever it rolls up a fat corporate surplus, it will have the daylights taxed out of it. . . . Think about this for a moment in the light of what we have found out about modern money, and you will recover from your surprise. If a corporation continuously returns its income to the spending stream, the dollar circuit is closed to that extent. If profits are high and dividends lush, then the individual who receives them is of course subject to the idle money tax. He must promptly spend or invest his dividends, or he will get the daylights taxed out of *him*.

The minute you hoard, down comes the guillotine! Will the plan work? I do not know. After an experimental period to shake out the bugs, it might. The turnover rate would have to be most carefully set, together with exact definitions of what constitutes spending and investment. Methods for camouflaging cash balances and beating the tax would have to be hammered out by experience—the way Milo Perkins hammered out the various tricks people thought of for getting around the food stamp plan.

Taxes on idle money, as proposed by Mr. Hazelett and Mr.

Dahlberg, are based on the assumption that money is a device, a means to an end, and that if men are going to use it they must respect its rules and keep the numbers moving. These plans also put a premium on venture capital for new enterprises. The premium has long been in reverse, forcing capital to be cautious and frigid. Under a different tax plan people might begin to take risks again the way they did in the nineteenth century. But we must not forget that the range of those chances will hardly be so wide in 1950 as it was in 1850.

It is important to consider whether a given new tax would be flexible enough to apply to periods of inflation as well as deflation. In general, a tax on idle money would seem more useful as a stimulant against depression, while a spendings tax (see page 93) might act as a sedative to quiet an overactive boom.

The tax lever in one form or another is absolutely cardinal in the compensatory system. It is the prime regulator of the dollar circuit, which in turn governs the businessman's prosperity or bankruptcy. We are here faced, however, with a serious psychological adjustment, as we noted earlier. Americans traditionally regard taxes as a burden and a waste, if not an outrage. But if they want a compensatory economy and not something much more radical, they will have to change their ideas and begin to think about taxes the way they have been taught to think about insurance. You pay now in order to avoid calamity later.

I do not know whether Americans can give up the man-in-the-barrel idea, and accept the insurance idea about federal taxes. It is going to be a difficult transition at best. The cartoon boys have done their work well. What I paid to the Collector of Internal Revenue on March 15th last, while far less than the price of one tank, would have been just cause for mounting the barricades a few years ago. I paid it, torn between horror and pride, as a contribution towards the defeat of the Axis. Will I pay as much, if necessary, towards the defeat of unemployment and social collapse when the war is over? I hope I shall have enough fortitude when the time comes.

Here is obviously another of those critical changes in outlook which Mr. Lippmann calls for. We are getting new thoughts about taxes now, staggering new thoughts. We must go on having them and getting used to them, little men as well as big. We clearly cannot hope to get through the demobilization period without new thoughts about taxes. We must have them for the stable and prosperous economy which lies beyond.

13

FULL EMPLOYMENT

Wʜᴇɴ ᴄʜɪʟᴅʀᴇɴ are shut up with nothing to do for any length of time, they are quite likely to start pulling the house down. When grown men and women are long deprived of useful work for their hands and minds, they are likely—if there are enough of them—to start pulling down the social order in which they live.

Chronic unemployment is not merely a question of labor wasted, production lost, relief measures, physical suffering, but of something even more fundamental. It is the question whether a biological specimen called man, with a nervous system designed for physical action, and a mind needing the respect of his fellows, can help running amuck when both these satisfactions are long denied him.

A "job" may or may not satisfy these timeless demands. Jobs are comparatively recent in the biological history of man. For most of his existence on this planet, he has been on nobody's payroll. He has worked for his livelihood on the natural environment about him in forest and field and sea, and always in relation to a tribe or group of which he has been an indissoluble member. It is a human instinct to crave the respect of that group; to want to belong and have one's place in it. Today, as an industrial hand, a man has lost the sense of personal responsibility for finding his food. He finds instead a piece of paper on payday, and exchanges that for things to eat and wear and live in.

At best, Station 14 on the assembly line is an indifferent substitute for the biological inheritance of man. But when even that collapses, and a man has nothing to do but pound the streets or sit waiting for nothing, then he might as well be dead. Nature, under the conditions of this earth, has no further use for him. If he turns on the gas with his last quarter, who can blame him? If he turns to a Hitler or a Huey Long to save him from this living death, who can blame him? Only people who know little of biology or psychology, and who have very limited imaginations, can blame him. Such people always can be recognized when they begin to raise their voices about bums and loafers.

Chronic unemployment is not amenable to casework methods. It is a sign of a profound social disease, a kind of cancer eating away at the foundations of the human community, as if the cells of the body politic were running wild, losing their order and structure. Temporary unemployment, like the care of the injured, can be handled by private charity, public relief, or some scheme of workmen's compensation—according to the enlightenment of the industrial civilization in which it occurs. When, however, a great mass of the able-bodied population is out of work for years on end with no hope in sight, the situation passes beyond any remedy by handouts or doles.

What Do We Mean by Full Employment?

If there are 60,000,000 Americans after the war who need

work to support themselves and their families, full employment as I understand it does not necessarily contemplate putting every last one of them to work on Monday morning.

First, we must deduct the "unemployables," those so handicapped physically or mentally that they cannot contribute a fair day's work for a fair day's pay. There may be a million such persons in the United States today. Many of them can do some work and are eager to, but if they and their families are to subsist on even a minimum level, a subsidy is inevitable.

Second, we must deduct "frictional unemployment," the quota temporarily idle because of business vicissitudes or shifting from one job to another, or because of the seasonal nature of their work, as in food canneries. In a work force of 60,000,000, a million or more would certainly be without employment at any given moment from frictional causes.

In 1929, before the crash, out of a working force of some 48,000,000, it was estimated that 2,000,000 were either unemployable or frictionally unemployed.

What We Mean by Mass Unemployment

By the early months of 1933 there were from 13,000,000 to 15,000,000 unemployed, close to one worker out of three. Millions more were on part time, with a job but not a living wage. It has been estimated that the idleness of the decade of the 1930's cost this nation 100,000,000 man-years of work. This is an appalling economic waste, yet it is less wasteful than the erosion of the human spirit which that dreadful decade entailed. In addition to those who were actually out of work, perhaps twice their number were haunted with the thought: "How long before I, too, become an outcast?" There was a time in 1933 when nine out of ten of the carpenters, painters, architects, engineers, masons, in the construction industry had nothing to do. Yet foolish people were still at large announcing that any worthy man who wanted work could find it, and implying that these architects and masons were moral delinquents.

Today, in 1943, not only are we back to 1929 levels, but an ominous shortage of man power is rapidly developing. Hours of work are being extended. Women are leaving their homes to work in factories and shops. Schoolboys are out helping farmers. Men who had retired from business are back at their desks. Most Americans have recovered function and status. They can hold their heads up for they belong to the community again. They have work for their hands, and the respect of their fellows. The 4,000,000 young men who in 1940 had no work and were not in school, are fighting on a score of fronts. But we must not forget that this was not the result of natural economic recovery. It took a war and $300,000,000,000 of government orders to achieve it.

Nor should we forget that when the opportunity for work came, the millions of our citizens on public relief seized it eagerly. The late William Hodson, commissioner of welfare in New York City, drove this point home:

Families prefer jobs with decent wages to public assistance. The fear that relief would pauperize the population and destroy work habits *has been dissolved by events*. There could not have been the enormous reduction in the relief caseload unless there was a willingness to work as job opportunities became available. . . . There is no unemployment today because the government needs every able-bodied man and woman for service either in the armed forces or as workers in industries providing the weapons.[1]

1. Quoted from Mr. Hodson's report to Mayor LaGuardia on January 14, 1943. *Survey Midmonthly,* February 1943.

Mr. Hodson had some millions of people on his relief rolls during the past ten years. In the middle of the depression he told me that the congenital "won't works" might number 5 per cent—one in twenty. Perhaps he would have reduced that figure when the caseload went down. At all events, his statement is an eloquent refutation of the bums-and-loafers school of thought.

Public Credit

In 1932, with the economic temperature close to zero, pulling tax levers would not have availed us much in the fight against mass unemployment. It could have warmed up some idle money, but not enough for real recovery. We were too far down. People were too frightened to spend or invest freely, and heavy taxes would have frightened them still more. The only recovery engine at the time was deficit spending by the federal government, with a vigorous use of the national debt to speed up the dollar circuit.

In a compensatory economy with a wide field for private enterprise, there will probably be times when the dollar circuit breaks open, and something more than tax adjustments will be required to close it. Consider, for instance, the financial upheaval implicit in a great shift from automobiles to helicopters as the favorite vehicle for family transportation; consider the shocks as handicraft house construction gives way to prefabrication in the factory, with consequent displacement of men and markets.

For these jars and shocks of advancing technology the government should be ready with public works or other programs to absorb the people thrown out of employment. The credit machine ought to be coupled to the tax machine for as long as the emergency lasts. There are three chief ways to obtain public credit:

First, the government can borrow from the banks, increasing the dollars in the system.

Second, it can borrow dollars already in the system from the public.

Third, it can create new dollars via its own central bank, and loan them for work-producing enterprises, without interest, on a strictly self-liquidating basis.

The first method is always to be avoided unless the emergency is very severe, as in 1932. Long pursued, such deficit financing leads to inflation. The second method avoids the danger of inflation, but of course increases the public debt. For fighting unemployment in the demobilization period, this method is far preferable to borrowing from the banks. The public will have plenty of money, as we have seen, and not many opportunities to spend it until normal markets are opened again and industry has finished retooling. Why not lend some of it to the government to finance public works? If some plan of forced savings is in effect on D-Day, and one probably will be, it might be wise to hold it through the demobilization period. Thus the government, in the war against depression, could obtain its funds without resorting to bank loans or ballyhoo campaigns.

The third method, of non-interest-bearing revolving funds, has been argued persuasively by many students of finance, but to my knowledge it has never been really tested. It is one of those inventions which, like a tax on idle money, are probably on the cards.[2] The government would create new dollars through its own bank, thus saving the interest paid to com-

2. See Arthur C. Holden, *Money in Motion,* Harper, 1940.

mercial banks. This money is then loaned to cities, states, conservation districts, housing authorities, which have prepared careful blueprints for essential public works. It is loaned on a strictly self-liquidating basis. The entire principal must be repaid over the life of the investment, so much amortized each year. But as no interest is involved, the money cost to the borrower is something like half of the usual cost of principal plus compound interest.

Such loans are not a burden on the federal taxpayer, and should not appear in the federal budget at all.[3] Losses might occur when the borrower could not amortize, but allowance could be made in the form of insurance or of a small discount reserved by the government as each loan is made.

The advantages of the method are obvious. It provides more direct employment per dollar of investment, and does not increase the national debt at all. It does increase local government debts, but on terms to make any city treasurer weep for joy. As the amortization payments come in to the Treasury, they can be used for other loans or they can be canceled. Canceling them forces dollars out of the system altogether, precisely as in the case of repayment of regular bank loans.

Mr. Berle's Banks

A variation of this method has been advocated by Adolf Berle, Jr., in his plan for a new system of investment banks.[4] These banks, which could be public or private or jointly controlled, would deal solely in long-term paper. Their distinc-

3. In the Swedish budget system they do not appear. See page 107.
4. Hearings before the TNEC, Part 9, 1940. See also Mr. Berle's book cited earlier.

tive characteristic would be the power to make loans *at selective rates of interest,* ignoring the "market" rate, and setting an appropriate rate for a given project.

Here, for instance, is the city of New York. Suppose that computations show it will need in the next ten years new hospitals costing $450,000,000. Suppose these were built and paid for in the usual way, with money borrowed at 3½ per cent, and repaid over a thirty-year period. This would mean that the city would have to pay close to a billion dollars for the hospitals, or more than twice their construction cost. If New York could not afford any such outlay at the time, sick people would have to be content with inadequate hospitals. Mr. Berle's banks, however, would be empowered to loan money to New York City to build hospitals, at one half or one quarter of one per cent. This would save so much in interest that the city could afford to go ahead with its program, let contracts, employ carpenters and plumbers, care for its sick.

These banks would handle self-liquidating projects for private borrowers and for the government, both federal and local. They would "quote any rate of interest which was necessary to get the work done." For nonprofit enterprises like hospitals, the interest rate would be close to zero. For housing projects it would also be very low, and thus enable us to build perhaps two houses instead of one, with the same money. For long-term loans to business enterprises, the rate would be higher, but low enough to give the small businessman a break. Obviously there is a nice problem here of setting the differential rates. Project A will be jealous of project B if it gets a better rate.

A compensatory economy needs a flexible credit system as

well as a flexible tax system, but their interrelations remain to be worked out. Perhaps a tax on idle money, as proposed by Mr. Hazelett, would provide the circuit with such momentum that public credit to alleviate unemployment would seldom be required. We cannot know this in advance, however. There is no wind tunnel for testing idle money tax machines. We have to fly them first to see what happens.

Whether or not we need public credit for alleviating unemployment, we shall certainly need it for self-liquidating public works in their own right—the hospitals, conservation projects, schools, harbor improvements, highways, and the rest, which a modern state demands. And we shall probably need it to help provide employment in the demobilization period.

The Interest Rate

The proposals for banking agencies charging selective interest, or no interest, warrant careful consideration. They are squarely on the trend curve. Interest rates have been falling all over the world for many years. Some students, including John Maynard Keynes, expect them to reach zero in a generation. Modern money is issued at the command of governments and central banks. You do not get it from a goldsmith in his cubicle, as you did in the fourteenth century. Why should governments pay interest on the funds they themselves create? There is no answer to this question except that they always have in recent years. *Fortune,* in the article cited in Chapter 10, makes no bones about it: "interest is an obsolescent tribute . . . and is one of the dynamic business man's costs." This is strong language, but it is straight along the road we are traveling.

Public Employment

When the government steps in to underwrite full employment, it has two major fields in which to operate without seriously competing with private business: public works and social security. The latter does not employ anyone directly, except the clerical and professional staff, but it can stimulate employment indirectly by the steady flow of purchasing power which benefit payments encourage.

The fiscal engine for social security should be taxation; for public works it should be taxation tempered with such credit devices as we have just discussed—at the lowest possible rate of interest, and at the farthest remove from borrowing at the commercial banks.

In *Goals for America* in this series, I devoted a chapter to public works, describing the varied and challenging opportunities for employment. I will not go over the ground again, but I should like to give some illustrations of local tasks, which I believe are very important.

Every town in the nation is sending its young men to war. In my little Connecticut town, with a total population of 1,750, 150 names already appear on the plaque in front of the old white Town Hall at Redding Center. These men—let us hope most of them—will some day come home to Redding, and a thousand towns like it. It is there, in their own home town, in their own state, that planning for employment should really begin. The people themselves should see to it that their own boys have a place in the community, perhaps using local draft boards as Mr. Patterson recommends. This would tend to decentralize the whole program, getting it away from Washington and down to the grass roots. Washington's task would be to finance worthwhile local projects.

Arizona as a Model

The state of Arizona has a local Resources and Planning Board.[5] You know Arizona: red rim rock, air like sparkling burgundy, mountains, cowboys, deep mine shafts, Indians, organ cactus, green irrigated valleys in bright yellow deserts. In 1941, the Arizona board began to draft plans for the future development of the state, especially projects that could be set on foot immediately after the war "when profound readjustments will be necessary because of the return of men from the armed forces to the state."

What does Arizona need to become a better state to live in, and how can her returning soldiers contribute to that end? She needs many things, some of them very badly. Above all she needs *water,* the life blood of the dry Southwest. Half of her best farmland is now desert because irrigation does not reach it. There is a lot of water in the Colorado River below Boulder Dam. A series of dams and canals could bring it to regions where it is needed. Marginal land of low fertility could be taken out of cultivation and restored to pasture or forest. Many more permanent water holes are needed for the great herds of cattle and sheep.

Arizona requires a better crop pattern, as well as watered land. She ships out cotton, citrus fruits, melons, truck crops, beef, mutton, pork. She imports most of her dairy products and cereals. "Vast acreages now devoted to the raising of short staple cotton might better be utilized in raising other crops less dependent upon migratory labor, or more productive of assured incomes"—less specialization, more diversification and self-sufficiency. The guayule plant grows wonder-

5. Facts given are from the Board's mimeographed report to the Governor, January 15, 1943.

fully in Arizona. No matter how much synthetic rubber we may produce, we shall need some natural rubber like guayule to mix with it. Here is a fine field of development. Soybeans for plastics is another.

Arizona needs cheap electric power, both for her farms and for the new industries, the factories making plastics and alloys, which she hopes to establish after the war. Dams at Glen Canyon, Redwall, Bridge Canyon, have been planned to provide power, as well as to control floods, furnish irrigation, and energize a network of rural electrification lines. All of her ores are now shipped out of the state to be refined elsewhere. If she had the power, some could be refined at home, with a great saving in crosshauling. New industries will require new housing, public utilities, schools and recreation centers for the people who are to work in them.

Arizona desperately needs better control of erosion. Overgrazing, denuded forests in the mountains, flash floods, have started terrible gulleys. Some reservoirs are filling with silt. Erosion must be checked before it is too late.

Arizona would like to have three super highways crossing the full length of the state, sometimes four, sometimes six lanes wide. Her present highway system, meanwhile, is rapidly deteriorating, and will demand extensive improvements and resurfacing when cars have gasoline enough to run again. Recreation areas should be extensively developed, for the winter tourist traffic is one of the state's chief sources of income.

Large parts of Arizona form great natural flying fields. The aviation industry, in peace as well as war, could develop here both flying schools and aircraft factories.

Arizona needs better houses for her people to live in.

Slums, blighted areas, unspeakable conditions in the camps where migratory laborers squat, the Negro and Mexican quarters in the cities—all demand drastic improvement. She needs more housing authorities, and playgrounds, parks, swimming pools, recreation centers, in the cities. She needs more regular hospitals; plans are also being laid for a series of veterans' hospitals where wounded soldiers may be cured in the invigorating air of the Southwest. She needs more schools, especially vocational schools where returning soldiers may be retrained for civilian tasks, and where special skills can be taught to those permanently crippled or injured.

Finally, the city of Phoenix is just completing a comprehensive program for public works which will serve as a model for other communities in the state.

Grass Roots Planning

This is what I mean by local initiative. These projects are all aimed at a splendid future for a splendid state. There isn't a leaf-raking plan in the lot. Returning soldiers who participate in any of them should be impressed by the value and importance of the work they have to do.

Many other states and cities also have established planning authorities. Mayor La Guardia of New York has a shelf of postwar projects totaling more than $600 million. But a great deal more needs to be done in the way of local initiative. If Americans really want to preserve the principle of self-help here is a golden opportunity. Local communities should have their blueprints drawn, ready to go at the touch of a button.

Broadly interpreted, public employment may include three great classes of enterprise when the war ends.

First, continued government employment for the armed forces, war industries, and lend-lease shipments. The man power retained may well run to 5,000,000 as estimated earlier, and be the largest item for federal underwriting.

Second, outlays for regular public works neglected during hostilities, such as highways, hospitals, schools. Much of this can be locally financed, but some federal underwriting may be necessary.

Third, outlays for new projects designed to take up the slack in private employment, while building up the country. Arizona's plans for Colorado river water, irrigation, power, housing, an improved crop pattern, new industries, flying fields, retraining schools, super highways, come under this heading. So do the great projects of the National Resources Planning Board for large-scale housing, reconstructing cities for the power age, integrating the system of continental transportation, developing more river basins, as the TVA has developed the Tennessee.

There is no question whatever about the opportunities for useful, exciting work in tasks like these—work that is a million miles from boondoggling. There is little question that the techniques for financing such work are now within our reach, as the London *Economist* believes.

The only question is whether we have the courage and the common sense to do it.

Theodore White, correspondent in Chungking, recently conducted a poll among the officers and men of one of our bombardment squadrons in China.[6] The views of the airmen on the role of America in the postwar world were mixed.

6. Reported in *Fortune,* May 1943.

But their views on the home front were remarkably unanimous. Officers and men alike, having for the most part no jobs to go back to, insisted that our country must do everything possible, "even to the point of reorganizing the economic system, to prevent another depression, maintain purchasing power, and provide employment."

It may not be unreasonable to expect that before the war has run its course, ten to twelve million young Americans, in all the armed services, will be thinking like this. A compensatory economy as we have pictured it stops some distance short of reorganizing the economic system. If it can give the young men what they want, will the rest of us be justified in blocking it?

14

SOCIAL SECURITY

Next to employment, social security may be the most powerful mass demand in the postwar world. When a man has a good job his security is covered, to a degree. But what if he loses his job to a new machine, and it takes half a year to find another one? What if he falls sick, or is injured in an accident, or grows too old to work? What about the children in families that have no active breadwinner? What about mothers who have lost their husbands, and are too busy taking care of the children to leave home and go to work? What about widows and orphans who are not blessed with large blocks of preferred utility stock? What about the health and nutrition of the oncoming generation?

Social security is the name for a method by which an interdependent, specialized power age society insures the survival of its members. Some stern moralists say that weaker members should die off. This brand of "morals" originates in a false interpretation of Darwin. Even if it were workable among apes in a jungle, the mass of mankind, I am convinced, would not stand for it.

Security for every American, based on personal savings and investment, is utterly impossible. If each of us over ten years of age had a nest egg of $10,000 in bonds, the resulting debt would be a trillion dollars—a figure to make even the war debt look like small change. Social security benefits are far easier to administer than a public works program because they require less detailed planning. Furthermore, they penetrate to every hamlet in the land. You do not need blueprints, or contracts, or engineers.

Provision for workmen's compensation, old-age pensions, state health insurance, and the like, has been steadily gaining throughout the world for fifty years. It is as solidly on the trend curve as the development of the airplane. Sweden, Germany, Britain, New Zealand, Australia, Finland, have been pioneers in preparing and adopting such programs. Some of our states—especially Wisconsin—have for many years done likewise. In 1935 Congress passed a federal act providing for benefits on an unprecedented scale. Some 30 million Americans are now paying social security taxes deducted from their pay envelopes.

Three New Programs

Within the past few months, three ambitious new programs for social security have been proposed. Sir William Beveridge submitted his plan to Parliament in December 1942; Mr. Roosevelt transmitted the report of the National Resources Planning Board to Congress in March 1943, and I. A. MacKenzie, Pensions Minister of Canada, laid a far-reaching plan before the House of Commons in Ottawa.

The new and significant feature of these three plans is that *everybody is included.* They push the idea to its logical end, where every Britisher, every American, every Canadian, is entitled to the benefits automatically, whether he be a Duke, a Rockefeller or a crossing sweeper. You get them the way you get the right to walk on the public streets. The benefits constitute an economic base, insuring minimum subsistence for the whole community. The base is so low that while no one can starve on it, no one would be content to stay on it except during dire emergencies.

None of the three plans has yet been adopted, and probably never will be in the present form. Parliament, Congress and the Canadian House of Commons will amend them. They will not, however, dismiss them. There is too much public pressure behind them. We have an inkling of that pressure in the Townsend clubs clamoring for old-age pensions.

The major provisions of the three programs are:

Insurance against unemployment.

Old-age pensions for all.

Health insurance for all.

Workmen's compensation for injuries or death while on the job.

Protection for the blind, the deaf, and other persons chronically handicapped.

Family allowances—in the British and Canadian plans.

Family Allowances

Twenty-eight countries have now adopted some plan of family allowances. In certain cases the mother receives a regular allowance for each child born after the first. The new Canadian plan contemplates allowances on the order of eight to nine dollars a month for all children under sixteen. For a mother with five small children, this might run to $45 a month, a substantial addition to the family budget, the difference between squalor and decency, perhaps the difference between bringing up a gangster or a skilled machinist.

The average cash outlay per child in American middle-class

families has been estimated at $10,500, and the cash return at zero. "Figures may be generalized for any social class," says F. Emerson Andrews, "by considering that each child costs approximately as much as a *house* for the income group involved."[1]

Family allowances have two purposes: to rear a healthier race, and to increase the birth rate—which, like the interest rate, has been falling for many years in most western countries. The experience of New Zealand shows that family allowances are administratively practical. I believe that they are indicated for this country in the future, but that they will not be won without a good deal more thinking about the population curve than we have done yet. The principle is now being applied, however, with allotments for the dependents of men going into the armed services.

Winston Churchill is a strong supporter of family allowances. In his radio talk to the world on March 21, 1943, he said:

Well-thought-out plans for helping parents to contribute this life-spring [of population] to the community are of prime importance. The care of the young and the establishment of sound hygienic conditions of motherhood have a bearing upon the whole future of the race which is absolutely vital.

The effects of social security, at least on children, would not be very different from the effects of personal security. Take my own case for example. I belong to the great middle class in America. I was not thrown out on the street to make my own way in the world before I finished school. I never knew hunger or want. I had good food, good medical care, a secure home, until my education was completed. Then I was

1. F. Emerson Andrews, "Family Allowances for America?" *Proceedings of the National Conference of Social Work,* Columbia University Press, 1942.

firmly put on my own. Perhaps this protection was bad for my character, but it was duplicated by millions of children in the comfortable classes. It is not irrelevant to remember that these same classes have supplied most of our engineers, teachers, architects, scientists, statesmen, artists, writers, inventors and business executives. Does this imply that if children in the mass could be better protected the nation would have more or better engineers, scientists, statesmen, artists and inventors? It implies just that.

Rage in Berlin

When Sir William Beveridge released his famous report to Parliament, the spokesmen in Berlin evidently suffered from extreme shock. Nothing since the war began had drawn louder protests from the Nazis. They had promised a new order in Europe, with security for all—except for the people they did not like. Here was an Englishman promising complete economic security to every last man, woman and child in Britain, and specifying how to provide it, with figures to the decimal point. There was nothing vague about Sir William's promise. It did not square at all with Nazi doctrine about brutal plutocracies allowing their people to starve in depressions. The Nazis had banked heavily on that doctrine, and here it was exploding in their faces. The rage in Berlin knew no bounds.[2]

Sir William had not only done well by humanity, but had forged for the United Nations a most effective weapon of psychological warfare. The Nazis, who came into power largely through a mass demand for social security, are well

2. See *The New York Times* story, December 6, 1942, headed: "Nazis Show Fears of British Reform."

aware of the greater mass demand all over the world which is bound to follow the war. They want no competition in playing for it.

Financing the Benefits

Who is going to pay for these benefits? The citizen himself will pay for a good part of them, while he is healthy and at work. A regular fee will be deducted from his pay envelope, as in the case of our own social security payroll taxes. His employer will pay a part, again as in our own case. The government will pay for the rest of it out of general taxation. Family allowances, for instance, require direct subsidy. That is where the tax lever comes in again. From idle money, inheritances, high incomes, the government will draw the sums needed above direct contributions.

Benefit payments will be hot money direct to consumers; they are sure to be spent rapidly. Thus the money circuit can be speeded, and businessmen will have a dependable market for food, clothing, rents, medical supplies and other essentials. Employment should be stimulated throughout the system. A social security program alone, however, cannot be expected to close the circuit and maintain full employment. Sir William Beveridge is emphatic about the necessity of more direct stimulants, such as public works. He says:

Income security, which is all that can be given by social insurance, is so inadequate a provision for human happiness that to put it forward by itself as a sole or principal measure of reconstruction hardly seems worth doing. It should be accompanied by an announced determination to use the powers of the state to whatever extent may prove necessary to ensure for all, not indeed absolute continuity of work, but a reasonable chance of productive employment.[3]

3. *Social Insurance and Allied Services,* Macmillan, 1942.

Both elements are covered in the reports of the National Resources Planning Board submitted to Congress by the President. Social security is covered less completely than in the Beveridge plan, especially as to estimating costs. Projects for full employment are treated in a comprehensive survey, which includes long-range plans as well as plans for the demobilization period. It should be an invaluable source book when the time comes to prepare the actual programs.[4]

A social security plan which protects everybody abolishes the poorhouse, the bread line, the unspeakable "means test," whereby one has to prove destitution to receive benefits. It puts the quietus on

> Organized charity, cold as ice,
> In the name of a cautious, statistical Christ.

It is a profound application of true democracy. There are no untouchables any longer. Everyone is eligible on an equal basis, just as in the case of the public schools. This provision will doubtless be fought, as the public schools were fought a century ago, with bad biology and worse logic, but when the fight is over, people may wonder why they got so hot and bothered about such a reasonable and inevitable proposal.[5]

A comprehensive program of social security would make for a happier nation, a sturdier nation, a more intelligent na-

4. Early in June 1943, Senator Wagner introduced into Congress a social security bill which would include all Americans in unemployment compensation, old-age pensions, health and disability insurance, soldiers' compensation.

5. Sample of the opposition in a letter to *The New York Times,* March 19, 1943:

"The recommendations [of the N.R.P.B.] are socialistic in trend and impractical to the nth degree. It seems to me that they rest on a false assumption and that false assumption is in turn based on a fallacy. The average American does not want his life charted for him by the government. He doesn't want to bet on a sure thing. What he does want is an opportunity to build his own security free from the prohibitive and fettering restrictions that impractical theorists would try to impose upon him."

tion, and for a higher birth rate. It would make children economic assets instead of liabilities. It would help to keep the dollar circuit closed. It dynamites the propaganda of our enemies. Behind it is a smashing, relentless political mass demand that cannot be dammed up indefinitely.

Perhaps it would be better for us if we could find our security as our forefathers did, by the work of their own hands in a simpler society. Perhaps the power age will ultimately develop a pattern of decentralization where this is possible. Such a pattern has not developed yet. Most of us are caught in a world of great centralized institutions, corporate, financial, governmental, on which we are utterly dependent for our jobs, for our dividends, for the safety of our savings, for our health, if not for our very survival. In the present state of technology, we cannot go it alone. When depression comes, when a machine takes over our work, when our bank or insurance company fails, we may face oblivion. Social security is the cement which can hold the community together.

The Free Market

Implicit in any plan for a compensatory economy is the widest practical area for free competition. As we have seen, the area has been steadily restricted by cartels, monopolies, administered prices, restrictions of many kinds on production. How can the free market shake off some of these fetters and give the consumer the benefit of mass volume at low prices? *Fortune* believes that the government must take the lead.[6]

To accomplish this restoration, the individual must enlist the aid

6. Supplement to the December 1942 issue.

of the very power that has been harassing him, and whose intentions he instinctively mistrusts: the power of government. For in this age the inertia of industry itself allows it to drift in the direction of collectivism; and only the active and determined intervention of the state can exert enough power to stop it. Moreover, the balance of economic power was transferred to Washington during the 1930's and will probably stay there. The only realistic question is: to what use will that power be put? We therefore ask a more rigorous governmental policing of the free market. For unless it becomes a better policeman, the government will become a universal economic administrator; and we should then lose all economic freedom, with which our other freedoms are linked.

The antimonopoly activities of the Department of Justice as conducted by Thurman Arnold are thus warmly endorsed by *Fortune*. The editors propose that public utilities be treated as regulated monopolies. Competing telephone companies or water companies make no sense. It would depend on the circumstances whether government or private capital should operate them. But in other areas competition does make sense, and there monopolies should be dissolved. *Fortune* would have the government prevent restrictions of output based on patent monopolies, administered prices, trade association agreements, labor union featherbed practices, farm bloc pressures, and so on down the line. It challenges the Robinson-Patman act, the Miller-Tydings act, and the Webb-Pomerene act—which permits international cartels to form at the water's edge. It urges federal incorporation.

Fortune, in brief, would raise hell with business-as-usual, as practised for many years. In so far as the free market is the best protection for the consumer—and often it is, as Dr. Dewhurst points out—this trust-busting program is to be recommended. But just what area the state can sweep out for free competition after this total war has run its course, is a puzzling question. It is the more puzzling because the historical trend has been running strongly in the opposite direction. The area may be smaller than *Fortune* hopes for, but certainly a determined effort should be made to keep it as large as possible.

Summary of the Compensatory Economy

Day by day, hour by hour, the war is molding the postwar economic system. All of us are being conditioned to new habits, new behavior, new ways of looking at men, materials, money, taxes, debt. If the war lasts for many years, its momentum may render such a program as we have sketched inadequate and superficial. On top of it may come far more drastic physical controls derived from war experience.[7]

Nobody really knows how long the war will last, or how it will end, despite the owlish certainty of some of our military experts. I have taken 1946 as a date for calculating the national debt, but this may be wide of the mark. I think it is reasonable to suppose, however, that if the active phases of the war do not extend much beyond 1946, a compensatory economy can logically succeed them, and many onerous physical controls can be dropped—some on D-Day, some with the end of the demobilization period, as indicated in Chapter 11.

Such an economy provides a way to achieve employment with minimum government interference in the mechanics of production and distribution. It contemplates very little extension of government ownership, though government and business might exercise joint control over the synthetic rubber and other war plants now being built at public expense. A com-

7. For a sketch of such controls, see Carl Dreher, *The Coming Showdown,* Little, Brown, 1942.

pensatory economy leaves most of the direct administration to nongovernment agents—big business, little business, co-operative societies, nonprofit organizations such as clubs, churches, foundations, universities. This is the pattern of a "mixed economy," where government exercises only key controls, most of them financial.

Industry versus Finance

At this point we strike an important distinction which I hope to develop at length in a later book in this series. It is the distinction between private business as a producer of goods, and as a dealer in money and evidences of indebtedness, a distinction, in short, between the industrialist and the financier. As a matter of historical fact, most encroachments by the state have come in the financial department. Increasingly the government has taken over functions of banking, credit, social insurance, stock market regulation, the redistribution of income. Except in Russia, there has been little advance by the state into ownership and operation of the means of production.[8]

With eyes on the trend curve, my guess would be that businessmen who devote themselves to producing physical goods and services are not going to be hampered much in that praiseworthy undertaking. Plenty of profitable opportunity awaits them in the coming years. They have a huge place in a compensatory economy. But businessmen who devote themselves to the creation of dizzy financial structures, to making money by manipulating money, are likely to find slimmer and slimmer pickings. This area is being rapidly invaded by the

8. Strikes involving the war effort may temporarily force the government into the operation of certain plants or industries.

public interest, and the stars indicate no retreat. Thorstein Veblen forecast this trend as early as 1904, when he wrote *The Theory of Business Enterprise.*

The Best Hope for Private Enterprise

To succeed, a compensatory economy must have real give-and-take between government men, businessmen, labor men, and other organized groups. If we want to retain our economic freedoms, we shall have to do some sacrificing for them. Our loyalty must run first to the community as a whole, and only later to the Amalgamated Order of Cutters and Joiners, or to the General Widget Corporation. The war itself is pushing us in this direction. One by one the fingers of the pressure groups are being pried loose. The process is slow but I think inevitable.

A compensatory economy is certainly the only practicable hope of those who want a maximum of free enterprise. If even this seems to imply too much government interference, listen to the warning of Sir George Schuster, one of Britain's foremost businessmen:

We must have some measure of government control over the nation's commerce after the war. If each business seeks to run its own affairs according to its own single interest, I see little hope of avoiding rigid state control at every point. . . . The main problem is achieving a balance between the organizing power of the state, and the driving force of the free individual.[9]

In a compensatory economy, the state is responsible for full employment and social security. It is guided and checked by the measuring rod of a regular count of the unemployed. It relies heavily on taxation to keep the dollar circuit in active motion. Public works programs—such as those for Arizona—

9. *The New York Times,* November 25, 1942.

are on file ready for all emergencies, and the economy is also committed to a permanent program of public works in their own right and necessity. Through these and through social security legislation, it becomes possible to assure the budget of essentials—food, shelter, clothing, health services, education—to every American. A compensatory economy appears to be the next logical step. But it will not solve all our economic problems.

15

"NOTHING TO FEAR BUT FEAR"

Among the forces which have hitherto prevented an economy of plenty from steadily delivering the goods in peacetime are seven great fears. Few of us are free from them, though old people suffer more than young people, well-to-do people more than poor people. These fears are mostly in abeyance now, but they may come back to haunt us after D-Day.

Each of the fears is, or has been, legitimate. But when they fill our minds, they paralyze any positive action. If they were filling our minds now, we could not fight the war. If they fill our minds after the war, we cannot win the peace. We shall be too frightened to act decisively. We shall shut our eyes and hope for normalcy to save us, though normalcy is as dead as Warren Gamaliel Harding.

Here is a list of the seven fears, together with some answers to them which this book has dealt with. They have been in the back of my mind all the time I have been writing.

1. *The Fear of Inflation*

Many citizens, especially those on fixed salaries and incomes, are afraid that government underwriting of employment in peacetime will result in runaway prices that will reduce their scale of living, wipe out their insurance policies, render their savings valueless. They are haunted by the picture of the terrible German inflation of 1923.

If the government recklessly printed money to put the unemployed to work at tasks which created no new wealth, and kept on doing it, this fear would be realized. Kings and rulers have caused inflation thus in the past. But our knowledge of the dollar circuit now makes it clear that there can be no general inflation until full employment is reached. Meanwhile the war is teaching governments how to control inflation at the level of full employment. Shall we discard this knowledge and permit inflation to have its head—if indeed inflation rather than deflation is the immediate postwar danger? I cannot believe we are going to be as unrealistic as that. I doubt if those citizens who would like to scrap all war controls on D-Day are going to press their demands very hard when they realize what a resulting inflation might do to their own pocketbooks.

2. *The Fear of a Crushing National Debt*

People know that when their personal debts grow large enough they are forced into bankruptcy. They identify the public debt with their own, and lie awake nights worrying about national bankruptcy. Right now they are too busy worrying about ration cards and boys abroad to give much attention to the public debt, but many of them look forward to worrying about it when they have the time.

In Chapter 10 we have set forth certain reasons why this fear is largely groundless. Great nations do not go bankrupt in the way a person or business does because the debt they owe is to themselves. The chief dangers in a mounting debt are two: it may pump too many dollars into the system and thus stimulate inflation; it may cause trouble in the internal distribution of income by favoring the upper brackets against the lower. It is possible to control both dangers by a vigorous and well-planned use of taxes. If the price level is kept under control the public debt can be a great reservoir for public investment.

3. *The Fear of Bureaucracy*

If the government becomes responsible for full employment and social security, many citizens are afraid that a huge permanent staff of office holders will come to regiment us day and night, and gradually destroy our liberties. They fear the thin entering wedge which will bring complete government ownership. Once we start on this road, they are afraid that the end is Moscow.

This fear is perfectly legitimate. But people tend to make an absolute of it, as if they lived in a timeless world, not the actual world of 1943 to 1950. The purpose of a compensatory economy, as we have outlined it, is to *reduce* the bureaucracy, regimentation and restraints on liberties, from which we are already suffering in the war. I have tried to describe a postwar economy with controls at the minimum, consistent with full employment. The alternatives, I suspect, are those "rigid state controls at every point" which Sir George Schuster warned against. If the demand for full employment after the war proves to be indeed that driving political force which many of us expect, then we have to choose. The program I have outlined is the bureaucratic minimum.

If you fear Bureaucracy in the abstract, with a capital B, do not forget that the Telephone Company and the Pennsylvania Railroad, for example, have problems in bureaucracy very similar to those of the Post Office Department. It is impossible to operate any large modern organization without bureaus, clerks and officials.

4. *The Fear of Paternalism*

If government embarks on a welfare economy, it is feared that citizens will be so coddled and spoon-fed that they will lose their character and initiative. They will become soft and lazy, easy prey to tougher nations.

The Germans have a comprehensive system of social security which goes back to Bismarck. Yet German soldiers are said to be tough. New Zealanders also have had a welfare economy for many years. They were found to be even tougher than the Nazis when they helped to rush Rommel out of Egypt.[1] I have never seen convincing evidence that putting an economic base under the community weakens moral fiber, and I could cite plenty of evidence that the lack of it does. Modern slums are notorious breeding grounds for disease, degeneracy and crime. There would, of course, be danger in giving handouts to the able-bodied without requiring work from them. A program for full employment will have to be specifically designed to balance rights against duties.

5. *The Fear of the End of Progress*

This is a very common fear in America, though not so much in other countries. If the state collects taxes and savings for public works and welfare, what will be left for venture

1. A good brief account of the New Zealand system was given by Walter Nash, Minister from New Zealand, speaking before the Virginia Institute of Public Affairs, July 1942.

capital, and for the man who wants to build a better mouse-trap? Invention will die out. That progress which has been the hallmark of America will come to an end. We shall be reduced to one dead level.

If Congress has the wisdom to adopt incentive taxation, or something like it, this fear can probably be laid at rest. No more powerful device for promoting venture capital has ever been mapped. It would virtually force us to scour the country for mousetrap makers. The chief thing that worries me about it is that such gentlemen are not to be found behind every bush, now that most of our inventing is done in large corporation laboratories. But the tax equally stimulates investing in research, so if we do not get so much progress as we desire from inventors in attics and cellars, we may get it from the Bell Laboratories.

This fear, though a standard subject at businessmen's banquets, seems to me largely a myth. Material progress is not so much a function of freedom to invest as it is a function of a dynamic society. The Germans, man for man, are probably as good scientists and inventors as we are, yet their economy is, and has been, far from free. Furthermore, the fact that invention has been subsidized in great research organizations makes material progress inevitable, unless the organizations are broken up. Nobody to my knowledge has ever proposed to do this.

6. *The Fear That "What You Gain, I Lose"*

"If our initial impulses," says T. Troward,[2] "proceed from the belief that things are so limited that our gain can only come from someone else's loss, then we have here the root of

2. Bulletin of the Economic Reform Club of London, 1941.

envy, hatred and fear." The concept revolves around a fixed production—the idea that there is only so much output, or so much money. If somebody gets more of either, inevitably the rest of us get less. If the government spends money on public works, there is less to be spent on private works. The more taxes are taken to put the unemployed to work, the poorer we taxpayers must be. It is this fear which primarily motivates the economy bloc in Congress. Senator Byrd's remark comes to mind: "Cut government spending to the bone and then take the bone."

Many radicals and labor leaders hold a similar concept, but upside down. The more the rich spend for luxuries, the more miserable the budgets of the poor. But it is not the spending of the rich which does the damage, as we have seen, so much as their uninvested saving.

The idea of a fixed, limited product is very ancient and runs deep. It corresponded with the facts until Watt invented the steam engine. In handicraft societies, progress is normally so slow that total output *is* limited, and the more corn the baron takes, the less remains for the villager. Since the industrial revolution, with the use of inanimate energy, output per capita has multiplied itself many times. Our chief economic troubles in recent years have stemmed from surpluses rather than shortages. Somewhere there is doubtless a limit to the potential output of modern industry, but we have never reached it in peacetime.

The fear is expressed by both parties in most quarrels about wages. Managers are afraid that if labor gets more, stockholders will get less. Labor leaders are afraid that high profits mean low wages. Yet as early as 1920, Henry Ford began to preach and to practice the efficacy of high wages.

Many businessmen followed him in theory if not in practice. Low wages mean a low level of mass buying power, and low profits for businessmen as a group. Thinking in terms of the whole community puts a completely different face on the matter. The more wages, the more people will spend, and the greater the businessman's sales. Ford broke this fear by realizing that the better the wages he paid, the more cars he could sell. True, the principle may not work for one company alone, but it will work when all companies practice it together—up to the point of full use of the national resources.

Output now in the war is a conclusive answer to this fear. By releasing physical and financial machinery from cautious commercial habits, we are going to have a tonnage of goods in 1943 probably twice that of 1938. The first ceilings we are likely to hit in war production will be due to highly abnormal demand for special materials, and to the shortage of man power. In times of depression, the fear of financial limitations has an especially unfortunate effect. By believing that money is limited and that we cannot afford to put men to work, we have held output far below capacity, and thrown away the potential labor of the unemployed.

Despite its ancient and honorable origin, I sometimes think that this is the cruelest fear to which modern men can be enslaved. It was sound enough in 1800, but it has no relation to the technological and financial facts of the modern world. When the unemployed go to work, they gain and the rest of us gain too. Only when the economy is at maximum capacity has this fear any theoretical validity. But at maximum capacity we should be so deluged with goods that the fear would be unlikely to arise. It is a product of the age of scarcity.

7. *The Fear of the Masses*

Many well-to-do citizens are deeply disturbed about the effects of any proposed welfare program on the mass of the people. It is felt that the masses are not to be trusted. Unless they have the threat of starvation hanging over them they will not work. A special and dramatic case of this fear is seen in the South, where nearly every advance of the Negro is opposed because it is believed to threaten "white supremacy."

Modern biology has a complete answer to this fear, in its demonstration that there are no inferior classes. "Inferior" or handicapped individuals are found in all classes. But perhaps the decisive answer is found in the trend of history. Is a world revolution going on or is it not? I believe that it is. The "masses" can no longer be kept in their traditional places; they are on the march. Those who really cherish democracy are glad to see them marching. Those who dislike democracy will continue to be afraid. I have no arguments to give them, and no consolation to offer.

These seven great fears, in whole or in part, are the brakes that may hold back full employment when the war ends. No valid physical or financial reasons are now discernible on the horizon to hold it back. Balanced against these fears will be the terrible demand for work and for security from the men of the armed services, and the men and women of the war industries.

A book on how to finance the peace should perhaps be devoted primarily to overcoming fear. It would thus fall under the head of psychology rather than economics. I am only an amateur psychologist, but I know at least where the real difficulty lies.

The Great Hopes

More logical than the fears are the hopes of the postwar world. Here we stand on firmer ground. Here we say yea, rather than nay, and have the confidence to take positive action. Confidence is the key. One can name a score of men competent to find all the money we need to achieve full employment. The techniques are already forged or in process of forging. They know how to go about the task if we, the voters, will let them do it. There are men and organizations competent to administer social security programs and public works programs. There are men who know how to count the unemployed, how to design and collect taxation, and keep the national debt from getting out of hand. Are we going to let them do these things? Or shall we turn the economy over to trembling men, determined to do nothing? This is my major fear, but it does not often assail me. I believe too strongly in the common sense of my fellow citizens.

There is another, profounder reason which makes hope more logical than fear. Our economic troubles have been due to abundance, not to scarcity. Abundance, in the sense of capacity to produce, will be enormously advanced in America by the war. I find it difficult to be filled with gloom because we can produce so much. If another Ice Age were moving south, if the Black Death were upon us, if our crops were losing their vitamins to a dread new virus, I should be gloomy. But when the promise is for more and more material abundance, I refuse to succumb to more than temporary qualms. True, we have relied on disasters in the past to absorb our gigantic production. Now I believe we are compelled to face the problem and find a better answer.

A century hence, says John Maynard Keynes, there will be

no economic problem, even as there is today no problem of enough air to breathe. I believe him, and I might even lop fifty years from his estimate. Peter Drucker has already laid a wreath on the tomb of "economic man." He believes that the financial calculus of profit and loss is ceasing to be a mainspring for human behavior. The classic figure of economic man was a product of scarcity, when pennies had to be watched, and there was not enough to go around. He is increasingly out of his element in an economy of abundance.

It seems to me that the world is not only in a global war, but in the midst of a convulsive transition period, where human beings conditioned to scarcity are trying to adjust themselves to the technological facts of plenty. When the adjustment is made, they may look back on their worries and fears as one looks back on a bleak day in childhood; and wonder why they were so upset.

How long the transition will take is impossible to foretell, but there is no doubt that the war is quickening it by opening our minds to change—military, political and economic. Look at the speed with which types of arms are supplanted; the rising power of the land-based bombing plane, the decline of the battleship. And so with financial fears and fixed ideas. They too can be changed or supplanted.

Where does the money come from? It comes from the work of the people and the work of their machines. The war is forcing this lesson upon us. We may have learned it by Demobilization Day.